The History of
Mission San Juan Capistrano

The Jewel of the California Mission System

Created by: Logan Stover

Table of Contents

Introduction

Introduction

Welcome to "The History of Mission San Juan Capistrano," a journey through one of California's most iconic and historically rich sites. This book aims to take you, the reader, on an engaging exploration of the complete history of Mission San Juan Capistrano, from its earliest days to its present significance. Designed especially for teens and young adults, this book will offer a detailed yet accessible account of the mission's past, highlighting the people, events, and cultural changes that have shaped its story.

From the outset, it is essential to understand why Mission San Juan Capistrano holds such a special place in California's history. Founded on November 1, 1776, by Father Junípero Serra, it is the seventh of the 21 missions established by the Spanish along the California coast. The missions were integral to Spain's strategy to colonize and convert the native populations to Christianity. Mission San Juan Capistrano, in particular, became known as the "Jewel of the Missions" due to its picturesque architecture, productive agriculture, and vibrant community life.

Before the arrival of the Spanish, the area was inhabited by the Acjachemen people, who had lived there for thousands of years. This book will begin by exploring their rich culture and way of life, setting the stage for the dramatic changes that the Spanish colonization brought. You will learn about the Acjachemen's traditions, social structures, and the impact that the establishment of the mission had on their community.

As we delve into the history of Mission San Juan Capistrano, you will meet several key figures who played crucial roles in its development. Father Junípero Serra, a tireless missionary, envisioned a chain of missions that would not only spread Christianity but also create self-sufficient agricultural communities. His successor, Father Fermín Lasuén, continued this mission, overseeing much of the construction that still stands today. We will also highlight the contributions of Native American leaders and artisans who helped build and sustain the mission, often under challenging circumstances.

The mission experienced its golden era in the early 19th century, thriving as a center of agriculture, education, and culture. You will read about the innovative irrigation systems that supported vast fields of crops, the skilled craftsmen who created beautiful buildings and artwork, and the bustling daily life that made the mission a hub of activity. However, this prosperity was not to last. With Mexico's independence from Spain in 1821 and the subsequent secularization of the missions in the 1830s, Mission San Juan Capistrano faced significant challenges. The transition from a religious institution to a secular one brought about changes in ownership, purpose, and condition, leading to periods of neglect and decline.

Despite these challenges, the mission's story did not end. Efforts to restore and preserve Mission San Juan Capistrano began in the late 19th century and continued into the 20th century, transforming it into a cherished historical landmark. This book will guide you through the restoration efforts, the key figures and organizations involved, and the mission's rebirth as a symbol of California's rich heritage.

Today, Mission San Juan Capistrano stands as a testament to the resilience and enduring spirit of its people and history. It serves as a place of education, reflection, and celebration, drawing visitors from around the world. You will learn about its role in the local community, its educational programs, and the annual events that celebrate its legacy, such as the famous Swallows' Day Parade.

As you journey through the pages of this book, you will gain a deeper appreciation for the intricate tapestry of history that makes Mission San Juan Capistrano so unique. Each chapter is designed to provide a comprehensive understanding of the mission's past, enriched with historical facts, personal stories, and engaging narratives. Whether you are a history enthusiast, a student, or simply curious about the past, this book will offer insights and knowledge that will stay with you long after you turn the last page.

Join us as we explore the fascinating history of Mission San Juan Capistrano, uncovering the stories of the people who built it, the challenges they faced, and the legacy they left behind. This is not just a history book; it is a journey through time, offering a window into the lives and experiences of those who made Mission San Juan Capistrano what it is today. Welcome to the adventure.

Chapter 1
The Acjachemen

Chapter 1: The Acjachemen

Introduction to the Acjachemen (Juaneño) People

Long before the Spanish explorers set foot in what is now known as Southern California, the region was home to the Acjachemen people, also referred to as the Juaneño after their association with Mission San Juan Capistrano. The Acjachemen have a history that spans thousands of years, during which they developed a rich, complex culture that was deeply intertwined with the natural environment.

The Acjachemen's lifestyle was a harmonious blend of spiritual beliefs, social structures, and practical skills that enabled them to thrive in a region marked by diverse landscapes. Their culture was deeply rooted in their natural surroundings, and they exhibited a profound respect for the environment, believing that all elements of nature were imbued with spiritual significance.

Central to Acjachemen culture was their spiritual connection to the land and its resources. The Acjachemen practiced an animistic belief system, where every element of nature—animals, plants, rocks, and bodies of water—was considered to possess a spiritual essence. This belief system was reflected in their rituals, ceremonies, and daily practices. They worshipped a pantheon of deities and spirits, each associated with different aspects of the natural world. Ceremonies were conducted to seek blessings, ensure successful hunts, and maintain harmony with nature. These ceremonies often included singing, dancing, and offerings, and were led by spiritual leaders known as shamans. Shamans were revered figures within the community, believed to possess the ability to communicate with the spiritual realm and heal the sick.

The Acjachemen were organized into clans, each with its own distinct territory and resources. Leadership within these clans was typically hereditary, with the role of the chief, or "nókán," passed down through family lines. The chief was responsible for making decisions, resolving disputes, and leading the community in times of crisis. This role required wisdom, diplomacy, and a deep understanding of the clan's needs and resources. The chief was supported by a council of elders and advisors, who provided guidance based on their experience and knowledge. These elders were highly respected for their wisdom and played a crucial role in maintaining the social fabric of the clan.

The Acjachemen's economy was based on a combination of hunting, fishing, and gathering, with each activity finely tuned to the seasonal availability of resources. Coastal communities took full advantage of the rich marine environment, catching fish, collecting shellfish, and hunting sea mammals. Inland groups focused more on hunting terrestrial animals such as deer, rabbits, and birds. Gathering plant foods was a crucial part of their subsistence strategy, with women playing a central role in this activity. They collected a variety of seeds, nuts, fruits, and tubers, which were essential components of their diet. The acorn was particularly important, and the Acjachemen developed sophisticated methods for processing acorns into a nutritious flour. They also practiced controlled burning to manage vegetation and promote the growth of food plants, a technique that demonstrated their deep understanding of ecological principles.

Art and craftsmanship were highly developed among the Acjachemen, reflecting both practical needs and cultural expression. Basket weaving was a major craft, with women creating intricate baskets for various uses, from carrying goods to cooking and storage. These baskets were often decorated with complex geometric patterns and symbolic designs that reflected the weavers' artistic talent and cultural identity. Pottery was another significant craft, used for cooking, storage, and ceremonial purposes. The Acjachemen also made tools and weapons from materials such as stone, bone, and wood. These included projectile points, scrapers, and fishing implements, demonstrating their ingenuity and adaptability. The craftsmanship of these items was not only practical but also held cultural and spiritual significance, often being used in rituals and ceremonies.

The Acjachemen lived in villages composed of dome-shaped huts known as "kiiy," constructed from willow branches and tule reeds. These structures provided shelter from the elements and were well-suited to the local climate. Villages were strategically located near water sources and food supplies, facilitating efficient resource management. The layout of a village often included a central area for communal activities and ceremonies, highlighting the importance of social cohesion and cultural traditions. The construction of these homes demonstrated the Acjachemen's deep understanding of their environment and their ability to create sustainable living spaces.

Trade was an important aspect of Acjachemen life, facilitating the exchange of goods, ideas, and cultural practices with neighboring groups. They traded items such as shell beads, which were used as a form of currency, as well as foodstuffs, tools, and crafted goods. These interactions helped to create a network of alliances and fostered a sense of interconnectedness among different tribes. Trade routes extended throughout Southern California and beyond, highlighting the Acjachemen's role in a broader regional economy. These interactions were not just economic but also social and cultural exchanges that enriched the lives of the Acjachemen and their trading partners.

Ceremonial life was vibrant and integral to the Acjachemen's cultural identity. Seasonal ceremonies marked important times of the year, such as harvests, solstices, and other natural events. These ceremonies involved elaborate preparations, including the creation of special regalia, music, dance, and storytelling. Social gatherings were occasions for reinforcing community bonds and transmitting cultural knowledge. Storytelling played a crucial role in preserving history, teaching moral lessons, and entertaining both young and old. Elders were respected as the primary storytellers, ensuring that traditions and values were passed down through generations. These ceremonies and social gatherings fostered a strong sense of community and continuity, ensuring that cultural practices and values were upheld.

Education in Acjachemen society was largely informal and experiential, with knowledge passed down through observation, participation, and oral traditions. Children learned essential skills from their parents and elders, such as hunting techniques, plant identification, and craft making. Cultural knowledge, including language, stories, and spiritual beliefs, was also transmitted orally. This system of education ensured the continuity of cultural practices and the survival of the community's way of life. The role of the elders in this educational process was crucial, as they were the keepers of the community's history and knowledge.

Before the arrival of the Spanish, the Acjachemen people had established a thriving society characterized by a deep connection to their environment, sophisticated social structures, and rich cultural traditions. Their way of life was abruptly changed with the arrival of the Spanish missionaries, but the resilience and adaptability of the

Acjachemen people have ensured that their cultural legacy endures to this day. Understanding their culture, lifestyle, and traditions before Spanish contact provides essential context for appreciating the profound changes and adaptations that followed. This foundation of knowledge allows us to recognize and honor the enduring contributions of the Acjachemen people to California's history and cultural heritage.

Significant Locations and Artifacts

The Acjachemen people's deep connection to their land is reflected in the significant locations and artifacts that have been discovered and preserved in the region around San Juan Capistrano. These sites and objects provide valuable insights into their daily lives, spiritual practices, and cultural heritage, offering a tangible link to the past.

Village Sites Numerous Acjachemen village sites have been identified throughout Southern California, particularly along the coast and near water sources such as rivers and springs. These sites were strategically chosen for their access to resources and favorable living conditions. Excavations at these locations have revealed the foundations of their dwellings, known as "kiiy," as well as communal spaces where social and ceremonial activities took place. The layout of these villages often included a central plaza used for gatherings and rituals, underscoring the importance of community cohesion in Acjachemen society.

Rock Art and Sacred Sites Rock art sites, featuring petroglyphs and pictographs, are scattered throughout Acjachemen territory. These artworks, etched or painted onto stone surfaces, depict a variety of symbols, animals, and abstract patterns. The exact meanings of these symbols are not always clear, but they are believed to hold spiritual significance and may have been used in rituals or as markers of sacred spaces. Some rock art sites are associated with legends and oral histories passed down through generations, adding layers of cultural meaning to these enigmatic images.

Burial Grounds Acjachemen burial grounds are sacred sites where the remains of their ancestors were laid to rest. These burial sites often contain grave goods, including pottery, tools, and personal ornaments, which provide insights into the Acjachemen's beliefs about the afterlife and their practices of honoring the deceased. The careful preservation and study of these sites are essential for understanding the spiritual and cultural practices of the Acjachemen people.

Seasonal Camps and Resource Gathering Areas In addition to permanent villages, the Acjachemen utilized a network of seasonal camps and resource gathering areas. These locations were used during specific times of the year to harvest seasonal foods, such as acorns, seeds, and coastal resources. Archaeological evidence from these sites includes grinding stones, shell middens, and remnants of temporary shelters, illustrating the Acjachemen's resource management strategies and their adaptability to different environments.

Stone tools and weapons are among the most commonly found Acjachemen artifacts. These include projectile points, knives, scrapers, and grinding stones. Projectile points, typically made from chert or obsidian, were used for hunting and were crafted with remarkable precision. Grinding stones, or "metates," along with the accompanying hand stones, or "manos," were used to process plant foods such as acorns and seeds into flour. These tools highlight the

Acjachemen's craftsmanship and their knowledge of local materials and techniques.

Basketry was a highly developed craft among the Acjachemen, with women creating intricately woven baskets for various purposes. These baskets were made from locally sourced plant materials such as willow, tule, and juncus reeds. The baskets were often adorned with complex geometric patterns and symbolic designs, demonstrating both practical skill and artistic expression. Some baskets were used for everyday tasks like carrying water or storing food, while others were reserved for ceremonial purposes.

Acjachemen pottery, although less common than basketry, was an important aspect of their material culture. Pottery artifacts include bowls, jars, and figurines, crafted from clay and fired in open pits. These vessels were used for cooking, storage, and ceremonial purposes. The designs and decorations on the pottery provide insights into the aesthetic preferences and symbolic meanings in Acjachemen culture.

Shell beads and ornaments were significant not only as decorative items but also as a form of currency and a symbol of social status. The Acjachemen crafted beads from various types of shells, including abalone and olivella, which were then strung into necklaces or sewn onto clothing. These beads were traded with neighboring groups and were used in ceremonies and as gifts. The production of shell beads required considerable skill and knowledge, reflecting the Acjachemen's expertise in utilizing coastal resources.

The Acjachemen also made use of animal bones and antlers to create a variety of tools and implements. These included awls for sewing, fishhooks for fishing, and needles for basket making. Bone tools were often shaped and polished, demonstrating the Acjachemen's ability to work with different materials to meet their needs.

Musical instruments such as flutes, rattles, and drums played a vital role in Acjachemen ceremonies and social gatherings. These instruments were made from natural materials like wood, gourds, and animal hides. Music was an essential part of Acjachemen culture, used to accompany dances, rituals, and storytelling, thereby enhancing the communal and spiritual aspects of their society.

The Acjachemen people, with their rich culture, sophisticated social structures, and deep spiritual connection to the land, thrived in Southern California long before the arrival of the Spanish. Their way of life was a harmonious blend of practical skills, artistic expression, and profound respect for nature. The significant locations and artifacts they left behind offer a glimpse into their vibrant and dynamic society, providing valuable insights into their daily lives, spiritual practices, and cultural heritage.

Understanding the Acjachemen's culture, lifestyle, and traditions before Spanish contact is crucial for appreciating the dramatic changes that followed the establishment of Mission San Juan Capistrano. The resilience and adaptability of the Acjachemen people in the face of these changes underscore their enduring legacy. As we move forward in our exploration of the mission's history, it is essential to remember and honor the original inhabitants of the land and their lasting contributions to California's cultural heritage.

Chapter 2
The Arrival of
the Spanish

Chapter 2: The Arrival of the Spanish

Spanish Exploration of Alta California

The exploration of Alta California by the Spanish was a significant chapter in the broader history of Spanish colonization in the Americas. This period marked the beginning of profound changes that would reshape the social, cultural, and political landscape of the region. Spanish exploration of Alta California, the area that is now the state of California, was driven by a combination of strategic, economic, and religious motivations.

By the mid-18th century, Spain had established a vast colonial empire in the Americas, including parts of what are now Mexico, Central America, and South America. However, the northern frontier of this empire remained largely unexplored and unsettled. Spain's interest in Alta California was partly motivated by the need to secure its northern territories against potential encroachments by other European powers, particularly Russia and England. The Russians had already established a presence in Alaska and were expanding their fur trade operations along the Pacific coast, while the English were increasing their activities in the Pacific. To counter these threats, Spain sought to extend its influence and establish a series of missions, presidios (military forts), and pueblos (civilian towns) in Alta California.

Economic factors also played a crucial role in Spanish exploration of Alta California. The Spanish crown was interested in exploiting the region's potential resources, including agricultural products, minerals, and trade routes. The fertile lands and favorable climate of Alta California offered the promise of abundant agricultural production, which could support both the local population and the broader colonial economy. Additionally, Spain hoped to discover valuable minerals such as gold and silver, which had driven much of its earlier colonial expansion in the Americas. The establishment of trade routes and ports along the California coast was seen as a way to facilitate commerce and bolster Spain's economic interests in the Pacific.

Religion was another significant factor driving Spanish exploration and colonization efforts. The Spanish crown, in collaboration with the Catholic Church, aimed to convert the indigenous populations of Alta California to Christianity. This goal was part of a broader strategy to integrate native peoples into the Spanish colonial system, both spiritually and culturally. The establishment of missions, led by Franciscan friars, was central to this religious mission. The missions were intended to serve as centers of religious instruction, agricultural production, and social organization, facilitating the conversion and assimilation of indigenous communities.

The first recorded European exploration of Alta California was undertaken by Juan Rodríguez Cabrillo, a Portuguese explorer sailing under the Spanish flag. In 1542, Cabrillo embarked on a voyage along the Pacific coast, reaching as far north as present-day San Diego Bay, which he named San Miguel. Cabrillo's expedition marked the initial European contact with the indigenous peoples of California, but it did not result in immediate colonization.

It wasn't until the late 18th century that Spanish interest in Alta California was renewed. In 1769, the Spanish crown authorized an expedition led by Gaspar de Portolá, a military officer, and Junípero Serra, a Franciscan friar, to explore and establish settlements in Alta California. The Portolá expedition included soldiers, missionaries, and settlers, and it marked the beginning of sustained Spanish presence in the region.

The Portolá expedition set out from Baja California in 1769, traveling overland along the coast. The journey was arduous, marked by difficult terrain, scarce resources, and encounters with indigenous communities. Despite these challenges, the expedition successfully reached the site of present-day San Diego, where they established the first Spanish settlement in Alta California, the Presidio of San Diego. This marked the beginning of Spanish colonization efforts in the region.

From San Diego, the Portolá expedition continued northward, exploring the coastline and identifying potential sites for future missions and settlements. Along the way, they encountered numerous indigenous groups, each with their own distinct cultures and ways of life. The expedition recorded detailed observations of the landscape, resources, and native peoples, providing valuable information for subsequent colonization efforts.

Following the Portolá expedition, the Spanish established a series of missions along the California coast, beginning with Mission San Diego de Alcalá in 1769. These missions were strategically located to facilitate the conversion of indigenous peoples and to serve as centers of agricultural production and trade. Each mission was typically accompanied by a presidio, which provided military protection and helped maintain Spanish control over the region.

The establishment of missions and presidios was a gradual process, with new missions being founded over the following decades. By 1776, the Spanish had established several missions along the coast, including Mission San Carlos Borromeo de Carmelo, Mission San Antonio de Padua, and Mission San Gabriel Arcángel. These missions formed the backbone of Spain's colonial presence in Alta California, playing a crucial role in the expansion and consolidation of Spanish influence.

While the initial focus of Spanish exploration was on the coastal regions, efforts were also made to explore the interior of Alta California. Explorers such as Juan Bautista de Anza led expeditions into the inland areas, mapping the terrain, establishing trade routes, and identifying potential sites for future settlements. The exploration of the interior was driven by the need to secure Spain's territorial claims and to expand its economic and strategic interests.

The Anza expeditions, in particular, were significant in establishing overland routes from Mexico to California, facilitating the movement of settlers, goods, and livestock. These routes became vital arteries for the development of the region, linking the coastal missions with the broader Spanish colonial network.

The Spanish exploration of Alta California had far-reaching consequences for the region and its indigenous inhabitants. The establishment of missions, presidios, and settlements disrupted traditional ways of life, leading to profound social, cultural, and demographic changes. Indigenous communities were often displaced, and their populations declined due to disease, forced labor, and other factors associated with colonization.

At the same time, the Spanish introduced new technologies, agricultural practices, and livestock, transforming the landscape and economy of Alta California. The missions became centers of agricultural production, with fields, orchards, and vineyards supplying food and goods for both local consumption and export. The introduction of European livestock, such as cattle and horses, also had a significant impact on the region's ecology and indigenous practices.

The exploration of Alta California by the Spanish set the stage for the establishment of Mission San Juan Capistrano and the broader mission system. Driven by a combination of strategic, economic, and religious motivations, the Spanish sought to secure their northern frontier, exploit the region's resources, and convert indigenous populations to Christianity. The early expeditions, led by figures such as Cabrillo, Portolá, and Anza, laid the groundwork for subsequent colonization efforts, shaping the course of California's history.

As we move forward in our exploration of Mission San Juan Capistrano's history, it is essential to understand the broader context of Spanish exploration and colonization. The arrival of the Spanish marked the beginning of a new era, bringing profound changes to the region and its indigenous inhabitants. In the next sections, we will delve into the specific events surrounding the founding of Mission San Juan Capistrano and the initial interactions between the Spanish and the Acjachemen people, examining the complex dynamics that emerged as two distinct cultures came into contact.

Initial Interactions Between the Spanish and the Acjachemen

The initial interactions between the Spanish and the Acjachemen people were marked by a mixture of curiosity, tension, and mutual adaptation. When the Spanish first arrived in Alta California, they encountered a well-established and complex society in the Acjachemen. These early encounters set the stage for the profound changes that would follow the establishment of the mission system.

The first recorded contact between the Spanish and the Acjachemen occurred during the Portolá expedition of 1769. As the expedition moved northward from San Diego, they encountered various indigenous groups, including the Acjachemen. These initial encounters were often brief and tentative, characterized by cautious exchanges. The Spanish, unfamiliar with the local languages and customs, relied on gestures and simple trade to communicate.

The Acjachemen, for their part, were naturally curious about these new arrivals. They observed the Spanish with interest, noting their strange clothing, advanced weaponry, and unfamiliar animals such as horses and mules. Despite the language barrier, the Acjachemen were quick to recognize the potential benefits of interacting with the Spanish, including access to new goods and technologies.

One of the primary forms of early interaction was trade. The Spanish offered items such as glass beads, metal tools, and cloth, which were highly valued by the Acjachemen for their novelty and utility. In exchange, the Acjachemen provided food, such as fish and acorns, and other locally produced goods. This exchange of goods helped to establish a rudimentary form of mutual dependence, as both sides sought to benefit from the other's resources.

Trade also provided an opportunity for the Spanish to learn more about the Acjachemen's social structures, customs, and territories. Through these interactions, they gained valuable knowledge about the local environment and the resources available in the region. Conversely, the Acjachemen learned about Spanish technology and goods, which began to influence their own practices and tools.

As the Spanish spent more time in Acjachemen territory, both groups began to adapt to each other's presence. The Spanish introduced new agricultural practices and crops, such as wheat and barley, which were soon adopted by the Acjachemen. This agricultural exchange had a significant impact on the local economy and food production, leading to changes in the Acjachemen's traditional subsistence strategies.

The Spanish also introduced livestock, including cattle, sheep, and horses. The Acjachemen quickly recognized the value of these animals for food, labor, and transportation. Horses, in particular, revolutionized Acjachemen mobility and hunting practices, providing them with a new means of transportation that increased their range and efficiency.

Religion played a central role in the interactions between the Spanish and the Acjachemen. The Spanish were committed to spreading Christianity and viewed the conversion of indigenous peoples as a primary goal of their colonization efforts. Franciscan friars, who accompanied the Spanish expeditions, began to preach and teach the Christian faith to the Acjachemen.

The Acjachemen, who had their own deeply rooted spiritual beliefs and practices, were initially resistant to the new religion. However, the friars' persistence, combined with the material benefits offered by the missions, gradually led to some Acjachemen adopting Christianity. This process of religious conversion was complex and multifaceted, often involving a blending of Christian and indigenous beliefs.

Despite the opportunities for trade and cultural exchange, the initial interactions between the Spanish and the Acjachemen were not without conflict. The Spanish presence and their efforts to establish control over the land and its resources often led to tensions and misunderstandings. The Acjachemen were protective of their territory and wary of the Spanish intentions, leading to occasional skirmishes and disputes.

One significant source of tension was the Spanish practice of bringing in soldiers to protect their expeditions and settlements. These soldiers, who were often unfamiliar with indigenous customs and attitudes, sometimes acted aggressively or disrespectfully toward the Acjachemen. Such actions exacerbated existing tensions and led to episodes of violence and resistance.

Another critical aspect of the initial interactions was the impact of European diseases on the Acjachemen population. The Spanish inadvertently introduced diseases such as smallpox, measles, and influenza, to which the indigenous peoples had no immunity. These diseases spread rapidly through Acjachemen communities, causing high mortality rates and significant social disruption.

The loss of life and the accompanying social disintegration weakened Acjachemen resistance to Spanish encroachment and made them more vulnerable to the Spanish mission system. The devastating impact of these diseases cannot be overstated, as they fundamentally altered the demographic and social landscape of the Acjachemen people.

During these early interactions, both the Spanish and the Acjachemen formed observations and perceptions of each other that would shape their subsequent relationships. The Spanish often viewed the Acjachemen through the lens of their colonial and religious goals, seeing them as potential converts and laborers for the missions. They admired the Acjachemen's knowledge of the land and their resourcefulness but also believed that European civilization and Christianity would bring them greater benefits.

The Acjachemen, on the other hand, had a more nuanced view of the Spanish. They were impressed by Spanish technology and goods but also wary of their intentions and the potential threat they posed. They recognized the power dynamics at play and sought to navigate these interactions in ways that would protect their interests and way of life.

Despite the challenges and conflicts, some Spanish and Acjachemen individuals managed to build positive relationships. These relationships were often facilitated by intermediaries, such as indigenous interpreters who had learned Spanish and could bridge the cultural and linguistic gap between the two groups. Through these intermediaries, mutual understanding and cooperation were sometimes achieved, paving the way for more sustained and structured interactions.

The initial interactions between the Spanish and the Acjachemen were complex and multifaceted, involving a mix of curiosity, adaptation, conflict, and mutual benefit. These early encounters set the stage for the establishment of the mission system and the profound changes that would follow. As we move forward in our exploration of Mission San Juan Capistrano's history, it is essential to understand these initial interactions and the dynamics that shaped them.

The arrival of the Spanish marked the beginning of a new era for the Acjachemen people, one characterized by significant cultural, social, and economic transformations. In the next sections, we will delve into the founding of Mission San Juan Capistrano by Father Junípero Serra, examining how the mission system was established and its impact on the Acjachemen and the broader region.

Founding of Mission San Juan Capistrano in 1776 by Father Junípero Serra

The founding of Mission San Juan Capistrano in 1776 by Father Junípero Serra was a pivotal moment in the history of California. This event not only marked the establishment of one of the most iconic missions in the California mission system but also symbolized the broader Spanish efforts to colonize and Christianize Alta California. The mission's founding had profound and far-reaching implications for the region's indigenous populations, the Spanish colonial enterprise, and the cultural landscape of California.

Father Junípero Serra, a Franciscan friar, played a central role in the Spanish mission system in California. His vision was to establish a chain of missions along the coast of Alta California to convert the indigenous peoples to Christianity, integrate them into Spanish colonial society, and secure Spain's territorial claims against other European powers. By the time Mission San Juan Capistrano was founded, Serra had already established several missions, including San

Diego de Alcalá, San Carlos Borromeo de Carmelo, and San Gabriel Arcángel.

The strategic location of San Juan Capistrano was chosen carefully. It lay between the already established missions of San Diego and San Gabriel, making it an ideal site to facilitate communication and travel along El Camino Real, the Royal Road that connected the missions. The region was also rich in resources, with fertile land and a mild climate conducive to agriculture, which was crucial for the mission's self-sufficiency.

On November 1, 1776, Father Junípero Serra led a small group of soldiers, settlers, and indigenous converts in a solemn ceremony to found Mission San Juan Capistrano. The ceremony included the celebration of Mass, the ringing of bells, and the establishment of a wooden cross to mark the site. This momentous occasion was not only a religious act but also a declaration of Spanish sovereignty and a symbol of Spain's commitment to its colonial and evangelical mission in Alta California.

Following the founding ceremony, construction began on the mission's buildings. The initial structures were modest, made of wood and thatch, but they were gradually replaced with more permanent adobe buildings. The mission complex eventually included a church, a convent, living quarters for the priests, soldiers, and indigenous converts, workshops, and storerooms. The architecture of the mission reflected a blend of Spanish and indigenous styles, with elements such as arched doorways, red-tiled roofs, and thick adobe walls.

The mission's layout was designed to facilitate its dual purposes of religious instruction and agricultural production.

The central courtyard served as a communal space for religious ceremonies, social gatherings, and daily activities. Surrounding the courtyard were the various buildings that housed the mission's inhabitants and supported its operations.

Agriculture was the backbone of the mission's economy. The fertile land around San Juan Capistrano was used to grow a variety of crops, including wheat, barley, corn, beans, and vegetables. The mission also established orchards and vineyards, producing fruits such as oranges, grapes, and olives. These agricultural products not only fed the mission's inhabitants but were also traded with other missions and settlements, contributing to the region's economic stability.

Livestock farming was another important aspect of the mission's economy. Cattle, sheep, goats, and pigs were raised for their meat, hides, wool, and other products. The introduction of European livestock significantly altered the local ecology and traditional indigenous practices, leading to both economic benefits and environmental changes.

The mission also engaged in various crafts and industries. Indigenous converts were taught skills such as blacksmithing, carpentry, weaving, and pottery. These crafts were essential for the maintenance of the mission and produced goods that were used within the mission and traded with other communities.

The primary purpose of Mission San Juan Capistrano, like all the missions, was to convert the indigenous population to Christianity and integrate them into Spanish colonial society. This goal was pursued through a combination of religious instruction, daily prayers, and participation in the sacraments. The mission's church became the spiritual heart of the community, where Mass was celebrated daily, and religious festivals were marked with special ceremonies and processions.

Life at the mission was highly structured, with a strict daily schedule that included prayers, work, and religious instruction. Indigenous converts, known as "neophytes," were expected to adhere to this schedule and adopt Spanish customs and practices. The missionaries believed that by doing so, the neophytes would be better prepared for eternal salvation and a more civilized life.

Despite the missionaries' intentions, the imposition of Spanish customs and the disruption of traditional ways of life often led to tension and resistance. The neophytes were required to live at the mission, separated from their traditional lands and communities. This separation caused significant social and cultural dislocation, leading to a loss of traditional knowledge and practices.

The founding of Mission San Juan Capistrano had a profound impact on the Acjachemen people. The mission system disrupted their traditional way of life, as many Acjachemen were brought to live at the mission and converted to Christianity. This forced relocation and cultural assimilation led to significant changes in their social structures, religious practices, and daily routines.

The introduction of European agriculture and livestock also transformed the local environment and economy. Traditional hunting, gathering, and agricultural practices were replaced by the mission's farming methods, which altered the landscape and reduced the availability of native resources. This environmental change further contributed to the Acjachemen's dependence on the mission for food and supplies.

Health and disease were also major issues. The close quarters and new living conditions at the mission, combined with the introduction of European diseases, led to high mortality rates among the Acjachemen. Epidemics of smallpox, measles, and other diseases decimated the population, leading to a significant decline in their numbers and further weakening their social structures.

The founding of Mission San Juan Capistrano by Father Junípero Serra was a key moment in the history of California. It marked the expansion of the Spanish mission system and solidified Spain's presence in Alta California. The mission became a center of religious, economic, and cultural life, influencing the region for decades to come.

Mission San Juan Capistrano is often referred to as the "Jewel of the Missions" due to its historical significance, architectural beauty, and the richness of its cultural heritage. It played a crucial role in the development of the surrounding area, contributing to the growth of nearby settlements and the establishment of agricultural and trade networks.

Today, Mission San Juan Capistrano stands as a testament to this complex history. It is a symbol of the Spanish colonial enterprise and its lasting impact on California, as well as a reminder of the resilience and adaptability of the Acjachemen people. The mission is a cherished historical site, attracting visitors from around the world who come to learn about its history, admire its architecture, and reflect on its legacy.

The arrival of the Spanish and the founding of Mission San Juan Capistrano marked the beginning of a new era in the history of Alta California. Driven by strategic, economic, and religious motivations, the Spanish sought to extend their influence and secure their claims in the region. The initial interactions between the Spanish and the Acjachemen set the stage for the profound changes that would follow, as the mission system disrupted traditional ways of life and introduced new cultural, economic, and social dynamics.

The founding of Mission San Juan Capistrano by Father Junípero Serra in 1776 was a momentous event, reflecting the broader goals of the Spanish mission system and its impact on the indigenous peoples of California. As we continue our exploration of Mission San Juan Capistrano's history, we will delve deeper into the mission's development, its role in the region, and the lasting legacy of its founders and inhabitants. This chapter sets the foundation for understanding the complex interplay of cultures, ambitions, and transformations that shaped the mission's history and continue to influence its significance today.

Chapter 3
Building the
Mission

Chapter 3: Building the Mission

Construction and Architecture of the Mission

The construction and architecture of Mission San Juan Capistrano represent a remarkable blend of Spanish colonial design and indigenous labor, resulting in a site of historical and cultural significance. The mission's development over time showcases the adaptation of European architectural principles to the local environment and the incorporation of native building techniques and materials.

When Father Junípero Serra and his companions founded Mission San Juan Capistrano in 1776, the initial structures were modest and temporary. These early buildings were primarily made of wood and thatch, serving as provisional accommodations and places of worship until more permanent structures could be built. The need for rapid construction meant using readily available materials and simple construction methods.

The first priority was to build a chapel for religious services and a basic living space for the missionaries and soldiers. These early structures were functional but lacked the durability and grandeur that later buildings would achieve. The primary focus during this initial phase was to establish a foothold and begin the process of converting the local indigenous population to Christianity.

As the mission community grew and resources allowed, the construction of more permanent adobe buildings began. Adobe, a traditional building material made from a mixture of mud, straw, and water, was widely used in Spanish colonial architecture. This material was well-suited to the

California climate, providing excellent insulation against both heat and cold.

The process of making adobe bricks involved mixing the raw materials, forming them into rectangular blocks, and allowing them to dry in the sun. Once cured, these bricks were used to construct walls that were typically several feet thick. The thickness of the walls not only provided structural stability but also helped regulate indoor temperatures, creating a comfortable living environment.

The construction of adobe buildings required significant labor, much of which was provided by the Acjachemen converts. Under the supervision of Spanish overseers and skilled artisans, the Acjachemen learned the techniques of adobe construction, contributing their labor and local knowledge to the building process.

One of the most ambitious construction projects at Mission San Juan Capistrano was the Great Stone Church, an impressive structure that symbolized the mission's importance and the Spanish commitment to their religious and colonial goals. Construction of the church began in 1797 under the direction of Father José Francisco de Paula Senán, who sought to create a grand place of worship that would inspire awe and reverence.

The Great Stone Church was designed in the shape of a cross, with thick stone walls and a vaulted ceiling. It featured a large central nave, side chapels, and a bell tower that rose high above the surrounding buildings. The stone used for construction was quarried locally, and the building process required the expertise of skilled stonemasons and laborers.

The church's architecture was influenced by the Baroque style, characterized by intricate ornamentation, dramatic contrasts, and a sense of grandeur. Decorative elements included carved stonework, frescoes, and stained glass windows, all of which contributed to the church's beauty and spiritual atmosphere.

Unfortunately, the Great Stone Church was severely damaged by an earthquake in 1812, causing the bell tower to collapse and resulting in significant loss of life. Despite efforts to repair and restore the structure, it was never fully rebuilt, and the ruins remain a poignant reminder of the mission's history and the challenges faced by its builders.

The layout of Mission San Juan Capistrano followed a typical pattern seen in many Spanish missions, with a central courtyard or plaza surrounded by the main buildings. This design reflected the Spanish colonial vision of creating self-sufficient, orderly communities centered around religious and communal life.

The central courtyard, known as the mission quadrangle, was the heart of the mission complex. It served as a gathering place for religious ceremonies, social activities, and daily work. The quadrangle was often landscaped with gardens, fountains, and pathways, creating a serene and functional space for the mission's inhabitants.

Around the quadrangle were the key buildings that supported the mission's operations. These included the church, living quarters for the missionaries and soldiers, workshops, storerooms, and residences for the indigenous converts. The buildings were arranged in a manner that facilitated efficient movement and interaction among the different areas of the mission.

Several architectural features and innovations distinguished Mission San Juan Capistrano from other missions. One notable feature was the use of arches and arcades, which provided both aesthetic appeal and structural stability. The arcades, with their series of connected arches, created shaded walkways that were practical for the warm climate and added a sense of elegance to the mission's design.

The mission also incorporated elements of Spanish and Moorish architectural styles, such as decorative tile work, carved wooden doors, and wrought-iron details. These elements reflected the rich architectural heritage of Spain and added to the mission's distinctive character.

Another innovation at Mission San Juan Capistrano was the extensive use of irrigation systems to support the mission's agriculture. The missionaries and indigenous laborers built aqueducts, reservoirs, and irrigation channels to bring water from nearby sources to the mission's fields and gardens. This system of water management was crucial for maintaining the mission's self-sufficiency and supporting its agricultural productivity.

The construction of Mission San Juan Capistrano required a combination of skilled craftsmanship and intensive labor. Spanish artisans and craftsmen, including stonemasons, carpenters, and blacksmiths, brought their expertise to the mission, overseeing the construction and training indigenous laborers in various building techniques.

The Acjachemen played a critical role in the construction process, providing the labor needed to build the mission's structures. They were involved in tasks such as making adobe bricks, quarrying stone, mixing mortar, and constructing walls. The labor was often demanding and carried out under challenging conditions, reflecting the broader dynamics of the mission system, where indigenous labor was central to the mission's operations.

In addition to their labor, the Acjachemen contributed to the cultural and artistic aspects of the mission's construction. Their knowledge of local materials and traditional building techniques complemented the Spanish architectural vision, resulting in a unique blend of styles and practices. Indigenous artisans created decorative elements such as pottery, basketry, and textiles that adorned the mission and reflected their cultural heritage.

The blending of Spanish and indigenous influences is evident in many aspects of the mission's architecture and design. This fusion created a distinct and enduring architectural legacy that continues to attract admiration and study.

The construction and architecture of Mission San Juan Capistrano stand as a testament to the collaborative efforts and cultural exchange between the Spanish missionaries and the Acjachemen people. The mission's buildings, from the initial thatch structures to the grand Great Stone Church, reflect the evolution of the mission over time and the challenges and triumphs experienced by its builders.

The mission's architecture not only served practical purposes but also symbolized the Spanish colonial and religious vision for Alta California. The blend of Spanish and indigenous influences created a unique architectural legacy that continues to be celebrated and preserved today. As we move forward in our exploration of Mission San Juan Capistrano's history, the next sections will delve into the daily life at the mission and the role of agriculture, livestock, and craftsmanship in sustaining this remarkable community.

Daily Life at the Mission for Both the Spanish and Native Americans

Daily life at Mission San Juan Capistrano was a blend of structured routines, religious observance, and communal labor, all within a framework designed to support the mission's spiritual, economic, and social goals. The daily activities were organized to ensure the smooth operation of the mission, the spiritual development of its inhabitants, and the assimilation of the indigenous Acjachemen people into Spanish colonial society.

The daily routine at the mission was highly structured, with a regimented schedule that began early in the morning and continued until evening. The day typically started at dawn with the ringing of the mission bells, which signaled the beginning of morning prayers and Mass. Attendance at religious services was mandatory for both the Spanish missionaries and the indigenous converts, reflecting the central role of faith in mission life.

After morning prayers, the day's work began. The division of labor was organized according to age, gender, and skills, with specific tasks assigned to different groups within the mission. Men were generally responsible for more physically demanding tasks, such as construction, farming, and tending to livestock, while women engaged in activities like cooking, weaving, and caring for children.

Religion was at the heart of daily life at the mission. The Franciscan missionaries, led by figures such as Father

Junípero Serra and his successors, were dedicated to the spiritual education and conversion of the Acjachemen people. Daily religious observances included morning Mass, midday prayers, and evening vespers. These services were conducted in the mission church and were attended by all members of the mission community.

Religious instruction was an ongoing process, with catechism classes held regularly to teach the fundamentals of the Catholic faith. The missionaries emphasized the importance of sacraments, such as baptism, confession, and communion, as well as adherence to Christian moral teachings. Indigenous converts, known as neophytes, were encouraged to adopt Christian names, practices, and values as part of their integration into the mission community.

The mission operated as a self-contained community, with communal living arrangements that fostered social cohesion and mutual support. The neophytes lived in barracks-like structures known as "neophyte quarters," which provided basic shelter and accommodations. These quarters were typically arranged around the mission quadrangle, allowing for easy access to the central courtyard and other communal areas.

Spanish soldiers, craftsmen, and their families also resided at the mission, often in separate quarters from the indigenous population. The soldiers were responsible for protecting the mission from external threats and maintaining order within the community. Their presence underscored the mission's dual role as a religious and colonial outpost.

The social organization within the mission was hierarchical, with the Franciscan missionaries at the top, followed by Spanish settlers, soldiers, and finally the indigenous converts. This hierarchy was reflected in the division of labor, living arrangements, and access to resources. Despite these divisions, the mission aimed to create a sense of community and shared purpose among its inhabitants.

Work was an integral part of daily life at the mission, with all members of the community contributing to its upkeep and productivity. The labor was divided into various tasks essential for the mission's self-sufficiency and growth. Men were typically involved in construction projects, fieldwork, and tending to livestock, while women engaged in domestic tasks, textile production, and food preparation.

The construction of adobe buildings, maintenance of irrigation systems, and cultivation of crops required considerable effort and coordination. Indigenous labor was central to these activities, with the Acjachemen learning new skills and techniques under the guidance of Spanish overseers and skilled craftsmen. This labor-intensive environment not only supported the mission's economic activities but also facilitated the cultural exchange between the Spanish and the Acjachemen.

The process of cultural adaptation at the mission was complex and multifaceted. While the Spanish sought to impose their customs, language, and religion on the Acjachemen, the indigenous people also found ways to preserve aspects of their own culture and traditions. This cultural negotiation was evident in various aspects of daily life, from religious practices to social customs and labor routines.

Despite the mission's efforts to assimilate the Acjachemen, there were instances of resistance and adaptation. Some indigenous people continued to practice their traditional rituals in secret, maintaining their cultural identity amidst the pressures of mission life. Others adapted to the new circumstances by blending Spanish and indigenous customs, creating a unique cultural synthesis that reflected their resilience and adaptability.

Education was a key component of daily life at the mission, aimed at both religious instruction and practical skill development. The Franciscan missionaries taught the neophytes to read and write in Spanish, with an emphasis on religious texts and catechism. Literacy was seen as a tool for deeper religious understanding and integration into colonial society.

In addition to religious education, the mission provided training in various trades and crafts. Indigenous men and boys were taught skills such as carpentry, blacksmithing, and masonry, while women and girls learned weaving, sewing, and cooking. These skills were essential for the mission's self-sufficiency and also provided the neophytes with valuable abilities that could be used beyond the mission walls.

Despite the regimented and labor-intensive nature of mission life, there were also opportunities for socializing and celebration. Religious festivals and feast days were important events in the mission calendar, marked by special Masses, processions, and communal meals. These occasions provided a respite from daily labor and an opportunity for the mission community to come together in worship and celebration.

The most notable of these events was the celebration of saints' feast days, particularly the feast day of Saint John the Baptist, the patron saint of Mission San Juan Capistrano.

These celebrations often included traditional music, dancing, and feasting, reflecting both Spanish and indigenous influences. Such events fostered a sense of community and continuity, reinforcing the mission's religious and cultural values.

Healthcare at the mission was rudimentary but essential for the well-being of its inhabitants. The missionaries provided basic medical care, often using traditional Spanish remedies and practices. Indigenous herbal knowledge was also incorporated into the mission's healthcare practices, reflecting a blend of European and native medicinal traditions.

The mission's infirmary, or "hospital," served as the primary location for treating the sick and injured. Common ailments included respiratory infections, gastrointestinal issues, and injuries from labor. The introduction of European diseases posed a significant health challenge, with epidemics causing high mortality rates among the neophytes. Despite the limited medical knowledge of the time, the missionaries made efforts to provide care and comfort to the afflicted.

The daily life at the mission had a profound impact on the Acjachemen people. The structured routines, religious instruction, and labor requirements significantly altered their traditional ways of living. While the mission provided new opportunities for education and skill development, it also imposed a rigid social order and disrupted the Acjachemen's cultural and social structures.

The experience of mission life was varied, with some neophytes adapting to the new circumstances and finding ways to integrate their own traditions, while others resisted or struggled with the changes. The mission system sought to transform the Acjachemen into loyal subjects of the Spanish crown and faithful adherents of the Catholic Church, but this transformation was neither uniform nor unchallenged.

The daily life at Mission San Juan Capistrano was a microcosm of the broader Spanish colonial enterprise, reflecting the complexities and contradictions of mission life. The structured routines, religious observance, and communal labor were designed to create a self-sufficient, orderly community that advanced the Spanish goals of conversion and colonization.

For the Spanish missionaries, the mission was a place of spiritual and social experimentation, where they sought to mold the indigenous population into a new, Christianized society. For the Acjachemen, the mission represented both an opportunity and a challenge, offering new skills and knowledge while imposing significant changes on their traditional way of life.

As we continue to explore the history of Mission San Juan Capistrano, the next section will delve into the role of agriculture, livestock, and craftsmanship in sustaining the mission and shaping its legacy. Understanding the daily life at the mission provides crucial context for appreciating the broader historical and cultural dynamics at play, highlighting the interplay of adaptation, resistance, and resilience that characterized this unique period in California's history.

The Role of Agriculture, Livestock, and Craftsmanship in Mission Life

The role of agriculture, livestock, and craftsmanship was central to the sustainability and success of Mission San Juan Capistrano. These activities not only provided the essential resources needed for daily life but also facilitated the mission's economic self-sufficiency and growth. The integration of European agricultural practices, livestock management, and artisanal crafts into the mission system profoundly transformed the local economy and the lives of the indigenous Acjachemen people.

Agriculture was the backbone of the mission's economy, ensuring a stable food supply for the mission community and generating surplus produce for trade. The Spanish missionaries introduced a variety of crops that were not native to the region but thrived in the favorable climate and fertile soil around San Juan Capistrano.

The primary crops grown at the mission included wheat, barley, corn, beans, peas, and a variety of vegetables such as squash, tomatoes, and peppers. The introduction of these crops required new farming techniques, including plowing, planting, irrigating, and harvesting, which were taught to the Acjachemen by the Spanish.

The mission also established extensive orchards and vineyards. Orange trees, fig trees, and olive trees were planted, providing fruits and olives that were consumed locally and traded with other missions. Vineyards produced grapes for making wine, which was an important sacramental and commercial product.

A critical innovation in mission agriculture was the development of sophisticated irrigation systems. The missionaries and indigenous laborers constructed aqueducts, reservoirs, and channels to transport water from nearby rivers and springs to the mission's fields and gardens. This irrigation infrastructure allowed for year-round cultivation, even during the dry summer months, and significantly increased agricultural productivity.

The irrigation systems not only supported the growth of crops but also helped to transform the surrounding landscape, creating fertile plots of land where previously only arid terrain existed. This engineering feat demonstrated the mission's ability to adapt European agricultural practices to the local environment, ensuring a steady food supply and fostering economic stability.

Livestock farming was another cornerstone of the mission's economy, providing meat, dairy products, leather, wool, and other resources essential for daily life and trade. The introduction of European livestock had a profound impact on the local ecology and the traditional practices of the Acjachemen people.

The primary types of livestock raised at the mission included cattle, sheep, goats, pigs, and poultry. Each type of animal played a specific role in the mission's economy and daily life. Cattle were particularly important, providing beef, milk, hides, and tallow. Sheep were raised for their wool, which was used to produce textiles, as well as for their meat. Goats and pigs also provided meat, milk, and other products, while poultry supplied eggs and meat.

Managing the large herds of livestock required significant labor and organization. Indigenous converts, under the supervision of Spanish vaqueros (cowboys), learned the skills of herding, breeding, and caring for the animals. Pasture management was essential to ensure that the animals had sufficient grazing land, and the mission established large ranchos (ranches) where the livestock could roam and feed.

The presence of livestock also led to the development of new infrastructures, such as corrals, barns, and dairies, which were necessary to house and manage the animals. The by-products of livestock farming, such as manure, were used to fertilize the fields, creating a sustainable agricultural system.

Craftsmanship was a vital aspect of mission life, contributing to the construction and maintenance of the mission, as well as producing goods for daily use and trade. The missionaries introduced various crafts and trades to the Acjachemen, who became skilled artisans in their own right.

Construction and masonry were essential for building and maintaining the mission's structures. Indigenous laborers, trained by Spanish craftsmen, learned to make adobe bricks, cut stone, and construct buildings. This training included techniques for building durable walls, arches, and roofs that could withstand the local climate and occasional earthquakes.

The Great Stone Church, one of the mission's most ambitious construction projects, showcased the skills of these artisans. The church's stone walls, vaulted ceilings, and intricate carvings were a testament to the craftsmanship and labor invested in its construction.

Blacksmithing and metalwork were crucial for producing tools, hardware, and other metal goods needed for the mission's operations. The mission's blacksmith shop was a busy place, where indigenous blacksmiths forged tools for farming, construction, and daily tasks. They also produced items such as nails, hinges, and horseshoes, which were essential for maintaining the mission's infrastructure.

Carpentry and woodworking were important trades at the mission, providing the wooden structures and furnishings necessary for daily life. Carpenters crafted doors, windows, furniture, and wagons, as well as agricultural tools and equipment. The mission's church and other buildings featured beautifully carved wooden elements, showcasing the artisans' skills and artistic expression.

Textile production was another significant craft, with indigenous women playing a central role in spinning, weaving, and sewing. Wool from the mission's sheep was spun into yarn and woven into cloth, which was used to make clothing, blankets, and other textiles. The weaving process involved looms and other tools introduced by the Spanish, and the resulting textiles were often decorated with traditional patterns and designs.

Pottery and ceramics were also produced at the mission, providing essential items for cooking, storage, and trade. Indigenous potters learned to shape and fire clay to create pots, bowls, tiles, and other ceramic goods. These items were used within the mission and traded with other communities, contributing to the mission's self-sufficiency and economic activity.

The integration of agriculture, livestock, and craftsmanship into mission life had a profound economic and social impact. The mission became a self-sustaining community, capable of producing the food, clothing, tools, and goods needed for daily life. This economic self-sufficiency was essential for the mission's survival and growth, allowing it to support a growing population and engage in trade with other missions and settlements.

The skills and knowledge imparted to the Acjachemen through these activities also had long-term effects. Many indigenous converts became skilled artisans and laborers, contributing to the mission's success and gaining valuable abilities that could be used beyond the mission walls. However, this process of cultural exchange was not without its challenges. The imposition of Spanish agricultural and craft practices disrupted traditional Acjachemen ways of life and led to significant cultural and social changes.

The role of agriculture, livestock, and craftsmanship at Mission San Juan Capistrano was central to the mission's success and sustainability. These activities provided the essential resources needed for daily life, supported the mission's economic stability, and facilitated the cultural exchange between the Spanish and the Acjachemen.

The introduction of European farming techniques, livestock management, and artisanal crafts transformed the local economy and the lives of the mission's inhabitants. The skills and knowledge imparted to the indigenous population through these activities had a lasting impact, contributing to the mission's legacy as a center of cultural and economic development.

As we conclude Chapter 3, we have explored the construction and architecture of the mission, the daily life of its inhabitants, and the crucial role of agriculture, livestock, and craftsmanship. These elements together created a vibrant and dynamic community that played a significant role in the broader history of California. In the next chapters, we will delve deeper into the mission's golden era, its challenges and decline, and its eventual restoration and preservation, further uncovering the rich tapestry of its history.

Chapter 4

The Mission's Golden Era

Chapter 4: The Mission's Golden Era

The Mission's Peak in the Early 19th Century

The early 19th century marked the golden era of Mission San Juan Capistrano, a period of prosperity and growth that solidified its place as one of the most prominent missions in Alta California. This era was characterized by remarkable agricultural production, architectural achievements, and a flourishing community life that reflected the success of the Spanish mission system.

During the peak years, Mission San Juan Capistrano underwent significant expansion and development. The mission's infrastructure grew to accommodate an increasing population of both indigenous converts and Spanish settlers. New buildings were constructed, and existing structures were expanded or renovated to better serve the community's needs.

The mission compound, with its central quadrangle, became a bustling hub of activity. The construction of additional adobe buildings, including new living quarters, workshops, and storage facilities, reflected the mission's growing economic and social complexity. The architectural style continued to blend Spanish colonial elements with indigenous techniques, resulting in a distinctive and functional layout.

The population of Mission San Juan Capistrano grew significantly during this period. By the early 1800s, the mission was home to over a thousand neophytes, as well as a sizable number of Spanish soldiers, artisans, and their families. This diverse community created a vibrant and dynamic social environment.

The increase in population was partly due to the successful efforts of the missionaries to convert and integrate the local indigenous population. The Acjachemen people, who formed the majority of the neophytes, played a crucial role in the mission's daily operations and economic activities. Their labor and skills were essential to the mission's prosperity.

Agriculture flourished during the mission's golden era, transforming the surrounding landscape into a productive agricultural haven. The extensive irrigation systems developed in earlier years were expanded and improved, ensuring a reliable water supply for crops and livestock. The fertile fields and orchards produced abundant harvests, contributing to the mission's self-sufficiency and economic strength.

The mission's agricultural output included a wide variety of crops such as wheat, barley, corn, beans, and vegetables. Orchards yielded fruits like oranges, figs, and pomegranates, while vineyards produced grapes for wine-making. The successful cultivation of these crops not only fed the mission community but also generated surplus produce that could be traded with other missions and settlements.

Livestock farming reached its peak during this period, with large herds of cattle, sheep, goats, and horses roaming the mission's extensive ranch lands. The mission's ranchos were well-managed, providing meat, dairy products, hides, wool, and other essential goods. The livestock industry became a cornerstone of the mission's economy, supporting its agricultural activities and contributing to its overall wealth.

Cattle ranching, in particular, was highly successful. The hides and tallow produced by the mission's cattle were valuable trade commodities, sought after by both local and international markets. The mission's vaqueros, many of whom were indigenous converts, became skilled in managing the large herds and maintaining the ranch infrastructure.

The architectural achievements of Mission San Juan Capistrano during its golden era were impressive. The construction of the Great Stone Church, despite its tragic destruction in 1812, stands out as a symbol of the mission's ambitions and capabilities. Other significant buildings, such as the priests' quarters, the neophyte barracks, and various workshops, showcased the mission's architectural sophistication and practical design.

The mission's buildings were constructed using durable materials like adobe and stone, with careful attention to both form and function. Architectural features such as arched doorways, red-tiled roofs, and decorative elements reflected the Spanish colonial style, while incorporating local influences and materials. These structures not only served practical purposes but also embodied the cultural and religious aspirations of the mission community.

The economic expansion of Mission San Juan Capistrano during its peak years was driven by its agricultural success and the development of various crafts and industries. The mission produced a wide range of goods, including textiles, pottery, leatherwork, and metal tools. These products were used within the mission and traded with other communities, enhancing the mission's economic standing and fostering regional trade networks.

The mission's economic activities were organized and managed with a high degree of efficiency. The division of labor ensured that each member of the community contributed to the mission's productivity, while the administrative oversight by the missionaries maintained order and coordination. This economic model not only supported the mission's growth but also provided a framework for the broader mission system in California.

The social structure of Mission San Juan Capistrano during its golden era was complex and hierarchical, reflecting the mission's dual role as a religious and colonial institution. At the top of this hierarchy were the Franciscan missionaries, who oversaw the mission's spiritual, economic, and social affairs. Below them were the Spanish soldiers and settlers, who provided protection and expertise in various trades.

The indigenous converts, or neophytes, formed the base of this social structure. They were integral to the mission's operations, providing labor and participating in religious and communal life. Despite their crucial role, the neophytes were often subject to strict control and supervision, reflecting the broader dynamics of colonial rule and cultural assimilation.

Daily life at the mission was structured around religious observance, communal work, and social interaction. The mission's schedule included regular prayers, Mass, and religious instruction, alongside agricultural work, crafts, and domestic tasks. Social events, such as religious festivals and communal meals, provided opportunities for the community to come together and celebrate their shared faith and accomplishments.

Despite its prosperity, Mission San Juan Capistrano faced several challenges during its golden era. Natural disasters, such as the earthquake that destroyed the Great Stone Church, posed significant threats to the mission's infrastructure and community. Additionally, tensions occasionally arose between the Spanish authorities and the indigenous population, reflecting the underlying cultural and social frictions of the mission system.

Nevertheless, the mission demonstrated remarkable resilience. The community's ability to rebuild and adapt in the face of adversity highlighted the strength and determination of its inhabitants. This resilience was a testament to the mission's robust organizational structure and the collaborative efforts of the Spanish and indigenous people.

The golden era of Mission San Juan Capistrano left a lasting legacy that continues to be celebrated today. The mission's achievements in agriculture, architecture, and community-building set a standard for other missions in California and contributed to the region's development. The cultural and economic foundations laid during this period had a profound impact on the subsequent history of the mission and the broader region.

The prosperity and growth experienced during the mission's peak years also underscored the complexities of the mission system. While the mission provided opportunities for cultural exchange and economic development, it also imposed significant changes on the indigenous population, leading to both benefits and challenges. This dual legacy is an important aspect of the mission's history, offering insights into the broader dynamics of Spanish colonization and indigenous adaptation.

The early 19th century represented a period of unparalleled growth and prosperity for Mission San Juan Capistrano. The mission's success in agriculture, livestock farming, and craftsmanship created a thriving community that was both economically self-sufficient and culturally vibrant. The architectural achievements and expansion of the mission during this time stand as enduring symbols of its golden era.

As we move forward in our exploration of Mission San Juan Capistrano's history, the next sections will delve into the economic activities, including agriculture and trade, and the cultural and social life during this period. These aspects will further illuminate the complexities and accomplishments of the mission's golden era, providing a deeper understanding of its legacy and impact.

Economic Activities, Including Agriculture and Trade

The economic activities of Mission San Juan Capistrano during its golden era were the foundation of its prosperity and growth. Agriculture, livestock, and trade formed the backbone of the mission's economy, creating a self-sufficient community that could support its population and engage in extensive regional trade. The mission's economic success was due to a combination of innovative agricultural practices, effective livestock management, and strategic trading relationships.

Agriculture was the primary economic activity at Mission San Juan Capistrano, providing food for the mission's inhabitants and surplus produce for trade. The mission's fertile lands and favorable climate allowed for the cultivation of a wide variety of crops, which were essential for the community's sustenance and economic stability.

The missionaries introduced European crops that thrived in the California climate. The mission's fields were planted with staple crops such as wheat, barley, corn, and beans. These grains and legumes were essential for the mission's food supply, providing the primary ingredients for bread, porridge, and other staple foods. The cultivation of these crops required extensive labor, with indigenous neophytes working the fields under the supervision of Spanish overseers.

Vegetable gardens were also an important part of the mission's agricultural activities. The mission grew a variety of vegetables, including squash, tomatoes, peppers, and peas. These vegetables added nutritional diversity to the mission's diet and were used in a range of culinary preparations.

The mission's orchards and vineyards were another key component of its agricultural success. Fruit trees, such as orange, fig, pomegranate, and olive, were planted in the mission's orchards. These fruits were consumed fresh, preserved, or used in cooking. Olive trees were particularly important, as they produced olives for consumption and olive oil, which was used for cooking, lighting, and as a trade commodity.

Vineyards were established to produce grapes for wine-making. Wine was an important sacramental product for the mission's religious ceremonies and was also consumed as part of the daily diet. The surplus wine was traded with other missions and settlements, contributing to the mission's economic network.

Effective water management was crucial for the mission's agricultural productivity. The missionaries and indigenous laborers built sophisticated irrigation systems, including aqueducts, reservoirs, and channels, to bring water from nearby rivers and springs to the mission's fields and gardens. These irrigation systems ensured a reliable water supply throughout the year, even during dry seasons.

The irrigation infrastructure allowed the mission to cultivate crops more intensively and consistently, leading to higher yields and greater economic stability. The ability to manage water resources effectively was a key factor in the mission's agricultural success.

Livestock farming was another cornerstone of the mission's economy, providing meat, dairy products, hides, wool, and other essential goods. The introduction of European livestock had a transformative effect on the local economy and traditional practices of the Acjachemen people.

Cattle ranching was particularly significant at Mission San Juan Capistrano. The mission maintained large herds of cattle, which provided beef, milk, and other products. Beef was a staple food for the mission's inhabitants, while milk was used to produce dairy products such as cheese and butter.

Cattle hides and tallow were valuable trade commodities. Hides were processed into leather for making clothing, footwear, and other goods, while tallow was used for making candles and soap. The trade of hides and tallow generated significant income for the mission and helped establish its economic connections with other missions and settlements.

Sheep farming was another important aspect of the mission's livestock operations. Sheep provided meat and wool, both of which were essential for the mission's economy. Wool was spun and woven into textiles, which were used to make clothing, blankets, and other goods. The production of wool and textiles was a labor-intensive process that involved shearing sheep, spinning yarn, and weaving cloth. Indigenous women played a central role in these activities, using skills taught by the missionaries and Spanish artisans.

In addition to cattle and sheep, the mission raised other livestock such as goats, pigs, and poultry. Goats provided milk and meat, while pigs were raised for their meat, which was an important source of protein. Poultry, including chickens and turkeys, supplied eggs and meat for the mission's diet.

The management of these diverse livestock herds required significant labor and organization. Indigenous converts, trained by Spanish vaqueros (cowboys), became skilled in herding, breeding, and caring for the animals. The mission's ranchos, or ranch lands, were carefully managed to provide adequate grazing and shelter for the livestock.

Craftsmanship and industry were integral to the mission's economic activities, supporting both daily life and trade. The mission produced a wide range of goods, including textiles, pottery, leatherwork, and metal tools. These products were used within the mission and traded with other communities, enhancing the mission's economic standing and fostering regional trade networks.

Textile production was a major industry at the mission, involving the spinning, weaving, and sewing of wool and cotton. Indigenous women were primarily responsible for these activities, using looms and other tools introduced by the Spanish. The textiles produced at the mission included clothing, blankets, and other essential goods, which were used by the mission's inhabitants and traded with other settlements.

The production process began with the shearing of sheep, followed by the cleaning and carding of wool. The wool was then spun into yarn, which was woven into cloth using hand-operated looms. The resulting textiles were often decorated with traditional patterns and designs, reflecting a blend of Spanish and indigenous influences.

Pottery and ceramics were also important products of the mission's craft industries. Indigenous potters, trained by Spanish artisans, created a variety of ceramic goods, including pots, bowls, tiles, and other items. These ceramics were used for cooking, storage, and other daily activities.

The production of pottery involved shaping clay by hand or using a potter's wheel, followed by firing the pieces in a kiln. The finished products were often decorated with glazes or painted designs, showcasing the artisans' skills and creativity. Pottery and ceramics were essential for the mission's domestic life and were also traded with other communities.

Leatherwork and metalwork were crucial crafts at the mission, providing essential tools, equipment, and goods. The mission's leatherworkers, or tanners, processed cattle hides into leather, which was then used to make clothing, footwear, saddles, and other items. The tanning process involved cleaning and treating the hides to produce durable, flexible leather.

Blacksmithing and metalwork were equally important, with indigenous blacksmiths producing tools, hardware, and other metal goods. The mission's blacksmith shop was a busy place, where tools for farming, construction, and daily tasks were forged. Items such as nails, hinges, and horseshoes were essential for maintaining the mission's infrastructure and supporting its economic activities.

The economic success of Mission San Juan Capistrano was not only due to its internal production but also its participation in regional trade networks. The mission engaged in extensive trade with other missions, settlements, and indigenous communities, exchanging surplus produce, livestock, and crafted goods for items that were not locally available.

Trade among the California missions was an important aspect of their economic strategy. Each mission specialized in certain crops or products, creating a system of mutual support and exchange. For example, Mission San Juan Capistrano might trade its surplus wine and olive oil for goods produced at other missions, such as wheat from Mission San Diego or textiles from Mission Santa Barbara.

This inter-mission trade network helped ensure that each mission had access to a diverse range of goods and resources, supporting their overall economic stability and self-sufficiency. The exchange of goods also fostered a sense of cooperation and interconnectedness among the missions, contributing to their collective success.

In addition to trading with other missions, Mission San Juan Capistrano engaged in trade with nearby Spanish settlements and indigenous communities. The mission's agricultural and crafted goods were sought after by settlers, who provided items such as manufactured goods, tools, and luxury items in return.

Trade with indigenous communities was also significant, as these exchanges allowed for the acquisition of locally sourced goods and fostered relationships with neighboring tribes. These trade relationships were often complex, involving negotiation and mutual benefit, and played a role in the broader economic and social dynamics of the region.

Despite its prosperity, Mission San Juan Capistrano faced economic challenges during its golden era. Natural disasters, such as the earthquake that destroyed the Great Stone Church in 1812, posed significant threats to the mission's infrastructure and economic stability. Additionally, fluctuations in agricultural productivity and livestock health could impact the mission's output and trade capacity.

However, the mission demonstrated remarkable resilience in the face of these challenges. The community's ability to rebuild and adapt, coupled with its diverse economic activities, helped maintain its prosperity. The efficient management of resources, labor, and trade networks ensured that the mission could recover from setbacks and continue to thrive.

The economic prosperity of Mission San Juan Capistrano during its golden era left a lasting legacy that shaped the mission's history and the broader region. The mission's agricultural innovations, livestock management practices, and craftsmanship not only supported its own community but also contributed to the economic development of Alta California.

The skills and knowledge imparted to the Acjachemen people through their work at the mission had long-term effects, providing them with valuable abilities that could be used beyond the mission walls. The economic foundations laid during this period influenced the region's development and set a precedent for future agricultural and industrial practices.

The economic activities of Mission San Juan Capistrano during its golden era were integral to its success and sustainability. The mission's agricultural productivity, livestock farming, and craftsmanship created a self-sufficient community that could support its population and engage in extensive trade. These economic activities not only ensured the mission's prosperity but also facilitated cultural exchange and adaptation.

As we conclude this section on economic activities, we have explored the various aspects of agriculture, livestock, and craftsmanship that underpinned the mission's economy. These activities were essential for the mission's growth and stability, providing a foundation for its golden era. In the next section, we will delve into the cultural and social life during this period, further illuminating the complexities and achievements of Mission San Juan Capistrano's most prosperous years.

Cultural and Social Life During This Period

The cultural and social life at Mission San Juan Capistrano during its golden era was a dynamic and vibrant blend of Spanish colonial traditions and indigenous practices. This period saw the flourishing of a unique cultural milieu where religious observance, social organization, education, and festivities played central roles. The mission community was characterized by a sense of shared purpose and identity, even as it navigated the complexities of cultural exchange and adaptation.

Religion was the cornerstone of life at Mission San Juan Capistrano, shaping the daily routines, social structures, and cultural practices of its inhabitants. The Franciscan missionaries, led by figures such as Father Junípero Serra, were dedicated to the spiritual education and conversion of the Acjachemen people. This process involved regular religious instruction, participation in sacraments, and adherence to a strict schedule of prayers and Masses.

The day at the mission began with the ringing of bells at dawn, calling the community to morning prayers and Mass. These religious services were held in the mission church, a central and sacred space where the community gathered to worship. Morning Mass was followed by other religious activities throughout the day, including catechism classes, vespers, and evening prayers.

Participation in these religious observances was mandatory for both the Spanish and indigenous inhabitants, reflecting the central role of faith in mission life. The missionaries used these occasions to teach Christian doctrines, reinforce moral values, and foster a sense of communal identity centered around the Catholic faith.

The sacraments of baptism, confession, communion, and marriage were important milestones in the lives of the mission's inhabitants. These sacraments were celebrated with solemn ceremonies and were seen as essential steps in the spiritual journey of the converts. Baptisms were particularly significant, marking the formal entry of indigenous individuals into the Christian community.

Religious festivals and feast days were highlights of the mission's cultural calendar. These events were marked by special Masses, processions, and communal meals. The feast day of Saint John the Baptist, the patron saint of Mission San Juan Capistrano, was a major celebration that included a festive Mass, music, dancing, and feasting. These festivals provided a break from the daily routine and an opportunity for the community to come together in celebration.

Education was a key component of mission life, aimed at both religious instruction and practical skill development. The missionaries established schools where indigenous children and adults learned to read and write in Spanish, with a focus on religious texts and catechism. Literacy was seen as a tool for deeper religious understanding and integration into colonial society.

In addition to religious education, the mission provided training in various trades and crafts. Boys and men were taught skills such as carpentry, blacksmithing, masonry, and agriculture, while girls and women learned weaving, sewing, and domestic tasks. This education was intended to equip the indigenous population with the skills needed to contribute to the mission's economic activities and to promote cultural assimilation.

The social structure at Mission San Juan Capistrano was hierarchical, reflecting the broader Spanish colonial system. At the top of this hierarchy were the Franciscan missionaries, who oversaw the mission's spiritual, economic, and social affairs. Below them were the Spanish soldiers, settlers, and artisans, who provided protection and expertise in various trades.

The indigenous converts, or neophytes, formed the base of this social structure. They were integral to the mission's operations, providing labor and participating in religious and communal life. Despite their crucial role, the neophytes were often subject to strict control and supervision, with their movements and activities closely monitored by the missionaries and Spanish authorities.

Daily life at the mission was organized around a structured routine that included religious observance, work, and communal activities. The day typically began with morning prayers and Mass, followed by a period of work in the fields, workshops, or other areas of the mission. Midday prayers and meals provided a break, after which work resumed until the evening.

Communal meals were an important aspect of daily life, reinforcing the sense of community and shared purpose. The main meal of the day, typically served at midday, included food produced at the mission, such as bread, vegetables, meat, and dairy products. These meals were eaten together in a communal dining area, fostering social bonds and a sense of unity.

Festivals and celebrations were key aspects of social life at the mission, providing opportunities for communal joy and cultural expression. Religious festivals, such as Christmas, Easter, and the feast days of saints, were marked by special ceremonies, music, dancing, and feasting. These events were occasions for the entire community to come together and celebrate their shared faith and achievements.

In addition to religious festivals, the mission celebrated various secular events, such as harvest festivals and trade fairs. These events often included games, competitions, and performances, adding to the vibrant social life of the mission. Music and dance played important roles in these celebrations, with indigenous and Spanish influences blending to create a unique cultural expression.

Music and dance were integral parts of cultural and social life at the mission. The missionaries introduced European musical instruments, such as guitars, violins, and drums, which were used in religious ceremonies and social events. Indigenous musical traditions also persisted, with traditional instruments and songs contributing to the mission's cultural diversity.

Dance was a popular form of entertainment and cultural expression, with both Spanish and indigenous dances performed at festivals and celebrations. The blending of these traditions created a rich and dynamic cultural landscape, reflecting the interactions and exchanges between the Spanish and indigenous communities.

Art and craftsmanship were also important aspects of mission life. Indigenous artisans produced a variety of artistic and functional items, including pottery, textiles, and woodwork. These crafts were often decorated with traditional patterns and designs, showcasing the cultural heritage and artistic skills of the Acjachemen people.

Healthcare at the mission was rudimentary but essential for the well-being of its inhabitants. The missionaries provided basic medical care, often using traditional Spanish remedies and practices. Indigenous herbal knowledge was also incorporated into the mission's healthcare practices, reflecting a blend of European and native medicinal traditions.

The mission's infirmary, or hospital, served as the primary location for treating the sick and injured. Common ailments included respiratory infections, gastrointestinal issues, and injuries from labor. The introduction of European diseases posed a significant health challenge, with epidemics causing high mortality rates among the neophytes. Despite the limited medical knowledge of the time, the missionaries made efforts to provide care and comfort to the afflicted.

The process of cultural adaptation at the mission was complex and multifaceted. While the Spanish sought to impose their customs, language, and religion on the Acjachemen, the indigenous people also found ways to preserve aspects of their own culture and traditions. This cultural negotiation was evident in various aspects of daily life, from religious practices to social customs and labor routines.

Despite the mission's efforts to assimilate the Acjachemen, there were instances of resistance and adaptation. Some indigenous people continued to practice their traditional rituals in secret, maintaining their cultural identity amidst the pressures of mission life. Others adapted to the new circumstances by blending Spanish and indigenous customs, creating a unique cultural synthesis that reflected their resilience and adaptability.

The mission environment fostered a variety of interpersonal relationships and social bonds. Family units were central to the mission community, with families living together in the neophyte quarters. These family bonds provided emotional support and stability, helping individuals navigate the challenges of mission life.

Friendships and social networks extended beyond family ties, with individuals forming connections based on shared experiences, work, and religious practices. These social bonds were reinforced through communal activities, festivals, and daily interactions, creating a sense of solidarity and mutual support.

The cultural and social life at Mission San Juan Capistrano had a profound impact on the Acjachemen people. The structured routines, religious instruction, and communal living arrangements significantly altered their traditional ways of life. While the mission provided new opportunities for education, skill development, and social interaction, it also imposed a rigid social order and disrupted the Acjachemen's cultural and social structures.

The experience of mission life was varied, with some neophytes adapting to the new circumstances and finding ways to integrate their own traditions, while others resisted or struggled with the changes. The mission system sought to transform the Acjachemen into loyal subjects of the Spanish crown and faithful adherents of the Catholic Church, but this transformation was neither uniform nor unchallenged.

The cultural and social life at Mission San Juan Capistrano during its golden era left a lasting legacy that continues to be celebrated today. The mission's achievements in fostering a vibrant community, blending diverse cultural traditions, and creating a unique social environment are an integral part of its history.

The resilience and adaptability of the Acjachemen people, their contributions to the mission's success, and their ability to navigate the complexities of cultural exchange and adaptation are key aspects of this legacy. The cultural and social dynamics of mission life offer valuable insights into the broader history of Spanish colonization and indigenous adaptation in California.

The cultural and social life at Mission San Juan Capistrano during its golden era was characterized by a rich tapestry of religious observance, social organization, education, and communal activities. The mission community was a dynamic and vibrant environment where Spanish and indigenous traditions blended, creating a unique cultural milieu.

As we conclude Chapter 4, we have explored the mission's peak in the early 19th century, its economic activities, and the cultural and social life that defined this period. These elements together created a thriving

Chapter 5

Decline and Secularization

Chapter 5: Decline and Secularization

Mexican Independence and the Secularization of the Missions

The decline and secularization of the missions in California were deeply intertwined with the political upheavals and transformations that accompanied Mexican independence. These changes marked the end of the mission system as it had been established by the Spanish and ushered in a new era of governance, property distribution, and cultural shifts.

In the early 19th century, the Spanish colonial empire in the Americas faced increasing challenges from both internal discontent and external pressures. The colonies, including New Spain (which encompassed present-day Mexico and California), were influenced by the broader movements of independence and liberalism that were sweeping through the Americas and Europe.

In 1810, the Mexican War of Independence began, led by figures such as Miguel Hidalgo and José María Morelos. This prolonged struggle against Spanish rule was driven by a combination of economic grievances, social inequalities, and the desire for political autonomy. The war lasted for more than a decade, causing significant disruption and instability throughout the region.

In 1821, Mexico finally achieved independence from Spain. The newly established Mexican government faced the daunting task of consolidating control over a vast and diverse territory. One of the key issues that the Mexican authorities had to address was the future of the Spanish mission system in Alta California.

The secularization of the missions was a process that aimed to transfer the control and ownership of mission lands and properties from the Franciscan missionaries to the secular authorities and private individuals. The rationale behind secularization was multifaceted, encompassing economic, political, and social objectives.

The Mexican government viewed the mission lands as valuable assets that could be redistributed to encourage settlement and development. By transferring these lands to private ownership, the authorities hoped to stimulate the local economy and integrate Alta California more fully into the national framework. Additionally, secularization was seen as a way to reduce the influence of the Catholic Church and promote a more secular, liberal state.

In 1833, the Mexican Congress passed the Secularization Law, formally initiating the process of secularizing the missions. The law outlined the redistribution of mission lands and properties, with the intent of returning some lands to the indigenous populations, granting parcels to settlers and soldiers, and converting the remaining properties into public assets.

The implementation of secularization varied across different missions and regions. In some cases, the process was relatively orderly, with the authorities overseeing the transfer of lands and properties in accordance with the law. In other instances, the process was chaotic and fraught with disputes and conflicts.

At each mission, the secularization process involved a detailed inventory of mission assets, including buildings, agricultural lands, livestock, tools, and other goods. The mission properties were then divided into parcels, which were distributed to various recipients. Indigenous neophytes were supposed to receive a portion of the land to support their continued livelihoods, although in practice, many indigenous people were marginalized in the distribution process.

The secularization of Mission San Juan Capistrano began in 1834, following the general timeline set by the Mexican authorities. The transition from mission control to secular administration involved significant changes in the management and use of the mission's resources. The secular authorities appointed administrators to oversee the process, ensuring that the mission's assets were inventoried and redistributed according to the new regulations.

The secularization process faced numerous challenges and conflicts. The transfer of land and property ownership was often complicated by competing claims and interests. Settlers, soldiers, and local authorities vied for control of the valuable mission lands, leading to disputes and, in some cases, violence.

Indigenous communities, who were supposed to benefit from the redistribution of lands, often found themselves disadvantaged. Many indigenous people lacked the legal knowledge and resources to navigate the complex land claims process. As a result, they were frequently dispossessed of the lands that had been promised to them, exacerbating their marginalization and economic hardship.

The Franciscan missionaries, who had dedicated their lives to the mission system, were also deeply affected by secularization. Many missionaries were forced to leave the missions they had established and nurtured, leading to a loss of spiritual and community leadership. The departure of the missionaries left a void in the religious and social life of the mission communities, further contributing to the decline of the mission system.

The economic and social impact of secularization was profound. The redistribution of mission lands led to significant changes in the local economy, as new landowners implemented different agricultural and management practices. The decline in centralized mission control resulted in the fragmentation of agricultural production and a decrease in overall productivity.

Socially, the secularization process disrupted the established community structures at the missions. The neophytes, who had lived and worked at the missions under the supervision of the missionaries, faced a new reality of increased uncertainty and instability. Many indigenous people struggled to adapt to the changing social and economic conditions, leading to increased poverty and displacement.

The secularization of the missions was part of a broader political reorganization in Alta California. The Mexican government sought to integrate the region more fully into the national framework, promoting settlement, economic development, and political control. The redistribution of mission lands was intended to encourage the establishment of private ranchos and agricultural enterprises, which would contribute to the region's growth and stability.

However, the political reorganization also led to increased tensions between different factions within Alta California. The centralized authority of the Mexican government was often challenged by local elites, settlers, and indigenous groups, leading to a fragmented and contested political landscape. The secularization process exacerbated these tensions, as various parties competed for control over valuable land and resources.

The secularization of the missions also precipitated significant cultural shifts within Alta California. The missions had been centers of cultural exchange and adaptation, where indigenous traditions blended with Spanish colonial practices to create a unique cultural milieu. With the decline of the missions, many of these hybrid cultural practices began to wane.

Indigenous communities faced the challenge of preserving their cultural identity in the face of increasing marginalization and assimilation pressures. The loss of the missions, which had served as centers of education, religious instruction, and social organization, left a void in the cultural landscape of Alta California.

The secular authorities, in their efforts to promote a more secular and liberal state, often downplayed or disregarded the cultural heritage of the indigenous population. This contributed to a broader process of cultural erosion and loss, as traditional practices and knowledge were overshadowed by the push for modernization and economic development.

The legal and administrative framework of Alta California underwent significant changes during the secularization period. The new Mexican authorities introduced laws and regulations aimed at restructuring land ownership and governance. These legal changes were intended to facilitate the redistribution of mission lands and integrate Alta California more fully into the Mexican state.

However, the implementation of these legal changes was often inconsistent and plagued by corruption and mismanagement. Local administrators and settlers frequently exploited the system for their own gain, undermining the intended goals of secularization. The lack of clear and effective legal mechanisms for protecting indigenous land rights further compounded these issues, leading to widespread disenfranchisement and displacement.

As mission lands were redistributed, the establishment of private ranchos became a defining feature of the post-secularization landscape. These large agricultural estates, owned by private individuals or families, played a crucial role in the economic development of Alta California. The ranchos were engaged in various agricultural activities, including cattle ranching, crop cultivation, and trade.

The rise of the ranchos marked a shift from the communal and religiously-oriented mission system to a more privatized and economically-driven land ownership model. The rancheros, or ranch owners, became influential figures in the local economy and politics, often exerting significant control over land and resources.

While the establishment of ranchos contributed to economic growth, it also led to increased social stratification and inequality. The concentration of land ownership in the hands of a few wealthy individuals contrasted sharply with the impoverishment and marginalization of the indigenous population and other lower social strata.

The secularization of the missions had a profound impact on the Catholic Church and the Franciscan missionaries. The loss of control over mission lands and resources diminished the Church's influence in Alta California. Many missionaries, who had devoted their lives to the spiritual and social welfare of the mission communities, were forced to leave their posts, leading to a sense of displacement and loss.

The secularization process also strained the relationship between the Mexican state and the Church. The Mexican authorities viewed the Church's extensive landholdings and influence with suspicion, seeking to curtail its power as part of broader secular and liberal reforms. This tension reflected the wider ideological conflicts of the period, as the newly independent Mexican state grappled with the challenges of nation-building and modernization.

The long-term consequences of Mexican independence and the secularization of the missions were far-reaching. The dismantling of the mission system marked the end of an era in California's history, leading to significant social, economic, and cultural transformations. The redistribution of land and the rise of the ranchos set the stage for the future development of California, laying the groundwork for its eventual integration into the United States.

The legacy of secularization is complex, reflecting both the opportunities and challenges of this transformative period. While the process aimed to promote economic development and political integration, it also resulted in the displacement and marginalization of indigenous communities and the erosion of cultural heritage. The story of secularization is a reminder of the profound and often contentious changes that accompany major political and social shifts.

The period of Mexican independence and the secularization of the missions was a time of profound change for Alta California. The transition from Spanish colonial rule to Mexican sovereignty brought with it new political, economic, and social dynamics. The secularization of the missions, driven by the desire to redistribute land and reduce the Church's influence, had far-reaching consequences for the region's development and the lives of its inhabitants.

As we move forward in our exploration of Mission San Juan Capistrano's history, the next sections will delve into the specific impacts of secularization on the mission and its inhabitants, examining how these changes affected the community and the use of mission buildings. Understanding the broader context of Mexican independence and secularization provides essential background for appreciating the complex legacy of this transformative period.

Impact on Mission San Juan Capistrano and Its Inhabitants

The secularization of Mission San Juan Capistrano had profound and far-reaching impacts on the mission and its inhabitants. This period marked a dramatic shift from the structured, communal life under the Franciscan missionaries to a more fragmented and uncertain existence. The effects of secularization were felt deeply by the indigenous neophytes, the missionaries, and the broader community, leading to significant social, economic, and cultural changes.

The transition from mission control to secular administration disrupted the established routines and social structures of Mission San Juan Capistrano. Under the mission system, the neophytes had lived and worked in a tightly regulated environment, with their daily activities centered around religious observance, agricultural labor, and communal living. Secularization dismantled this system, leaving many neophytes without the guidance and support they had relied on.

The departure of the Franciscan missionaries, who had been the spiritual and social leaders of the mission community, left a void that was not easily filled. The missionaries had provided not only religious instruction but also a sense of order and stability. Their absence led to a breakdown in the community's cohesion, as the neophytes struggled to adapt to the new secular authorities and the loss of their communal identity.

Secularization brought about significant economic hardship for the neophytes and other mission inhabitants. The redistribution of mission lands and resources often left the indigenous population at a disadvantage. Many neophytes, who had worked the mission lands for years, found themselves dispossessed of the very lands they had cultivated. The promises of land grants to the indigenous population were frequently unfulfilled, as local settlers and officials took advantage of the chaotic redistribution process to claim the most valuable lands for themselves.

Without access to land and the structured support of the mission, many neophytes faced severe economic challenges. They were forced to seek work as laborers on the newly established ranchos or in the towns, often for meager wages and under difficult conditions. The loss of the mission's agricultural and craft production also meant a reduction in the goods and services that had previously sustained the community, exacerbating their economic difficulties.

The social dislocation caused by secularization was profound. The mission had been a center of social organization and support, providing education, healthcare, and social services to the neophytes. The dismantling of the mission system left many indigenous people without these essential services, contributing to increased vulnerability and hardship.

The loss of communal living arrangements also had significant social impacts. The neophytes, who had lived together in the mission's quarters, were now scattered across the region. This dispersal weakened the social bonds and support networks that had been a key aspect of mission life. The sense of community and shared identity that had been fostered at the mission was difficult to maintain in the new, more fragmented environment.

Secularization also contributed to the erosion of cultural practices and traditions among the indigenous population. The mission had been a site of cultural exchange, where indigenous traditions blended with Spanish customs to create a unique cultural milieu. The loss of the mission as a cultural center meant that many of these hybrid practices began to fade.

The secular authorities often had little interest in preserving indigenous cultural heritage, focusing instead on economic development and assimilation. As a result, traditional practices, languages, and rituals were further marginalized. The breakdown of the mission community and the pressures of economic survival made it increasingly difficult for the neophytes to maintain their cultural identity.

The health and well-being of the mission inhabitants were also adversely affected by secularization. The mission had provided basic healthcare services, drawing on both Spanish and indigenous medicinal knowledge. With the departure of the missionaries and the decline of the mission's infrastructure, access to healthcare diminished.

The loss of the mission's organized living conditions and the economic pressures faced by the neophytes led to increased exposure to illness and poor living conditions. Malnutrition, inadequate shelter, and lack of medical care contributed to a decline in health among the indigenous population. The introduction of European diseases, which had already taken a heavy toll, continued to affect the community, exacerbated by the lack of coordinated healthcare.

The departure of the Franciscan missionaries meant the loss of religious guidance and support for the mission community. The missionaries had been central to the spiritual life of the neophytes, providing instruction, leading religious services, and administering sacraments. Their absence left a spiritual void that was not easily filled.

The secular authorities, who took over the administration of the mission, were primarily concerned with economic and political matters and often lacked the religious training and commitment of the missionaries. As a result, the religious practices that had been a core part of mission life began to decline. The neophytes, who had been accustomed to regular religious observance and instruction, found themselves without the spiritual leadership they had relied on.

The transition to secular administration brought new challenges for the mission inhabitants in adapting to the authority of Mexican officials. The secular administrators were often more focused on economic exploitation and less concerned with the welfare of the indigenous population. This shift in priorities led to a more exploitative and less supportive environment for the neophytes.

The new administrators frequently lacked the understanding and sensitivity needed to effectively manage the mission community. The indigenous population, already facing significant disruptions, now had to navigate a new and often unsympathetic administrative system. This lack of continuity and support made it difficult for the neophytes to maintain the social and economic stability they had experienced under the mission system.

The impact of secularization extended beyond the immediate mission community to the broader region. The decline of the mission's economic activities affected local trade networks and disrupted the regional economy. The mission had been a major producer of agricultural goods and crafted items, and its decline led to a decrease in the availability of these products.

The social and economic challenges faced by the mission inhabitants also had broader repercussions. The increased poverty and displacement of the neophytes contributed to social instability and tensions within the region. The breakdown of the mission's communal structures and support systems left a gap that was not easily filled by the secular authorities.

The long-term effects of secularization were deeply felt by the descendants of the mission inhabitants. The loss of land, cultural erosion, and social dislocation had lasting impacts on the indigenous communities. Many of the challenges faced during the secularization period continued to affect these communities for generations.

Despite these challenges, the resilience and adaptability of the indigenous population played a crucial role in their survival. While the mission system had imposed significant changes, it also provided skills and knowledge that could be used in new contexts. The neophytes' ability to adapt to changing circumstances and find new ways to support themselves was a testament to their strength and resourcefulness.

The secularization of Mission San Juan Capistrano marked a period of profound change and upheaval for the mission and its inhabitants. The dismantling of the mission system disrupted the established social, economic, and cultural structures, leading to significant challenges for the indigenous population. The loss of communal living, economic support, and religious guidance had far-reaching impacts, contributing to increased hardship and marginalization.

As we continue our exploration of Mission San Juan Capistrano's history, the next section will examine the changes in ownership and usage of the mission buildings following secularization. Understanding the impacts of secularization on the mission and its inhabitants provides essential context for appreciating the broader legacy of this transformative period and the resilience of the community in the face of adversity.

Changes in Ownership and Usage of the Mission Buildings

The secularization of the California missions brought about profound changes in the ownership and usage of the mission buildings, including those at Mission San Juan Capistrano. As the Mexican government implemented its secularization policies, the mission properties were transferred from ecclesiastical to civil control. This transition marked a significant shift in the function and condition of the mission buildings, reflecting broader social and economic changes.

Following the Mexican Secularization Act of 1833, the mission lands and buildings were subject to redistribution. The process was intended to repurpose the mission properties for public and private use, with a portion of the lands designated for the indigenous population who had lived and worked there. However, the implementation of these policies was often haphazard and marred by corruption and favoritism.

In the case of Mission San Juan Capistrano, the mission buildings and surrounding lands were divided and allocated to various individuals and entities. Secular administrators were appointed to oversee the redistribution, but their interests frequently conflicted with the welfare of the mission's former inhabitants. Large portions of mission lands were granted to influential settlers and government officials, while the promised land grants to the indigenous population were often delayed or never realized.

The mission buildings, which had once been centers of religious, educational, and economic activity, were repurposed for a variety of secular uses. Secular administrators took control of the main mission complex, including the church, living quarters, workshops, and agricultural facilities. These buildings were adapted to serve the needs of the new administrators and settlers, often with little regard for their historical and cultural significance.

Some of the mission buildings were used for government purposes, such as administrative offices and storage facilities. Others were converted into private residences or commercial establishments. The mission church, which had been the spiritual heart of the community, was sometimes neglected or repurposed for secular functions, leading to a decline in its condition and sanctity.

The transition to secular control resulted in a period of neglect and deterioration for many of the mission buildings. Without the dedicated care and maintenance provided by the Franciscan missionaries and the mission community, the buildings began to fall into disrepair. The secular administrators often lacked the resources or motivation to preserve the structures, and their new uses frequently contributed to their degradation.

The Great Stone Church, which had already suffered significant damage from the earthquake of 1812, was further neglected during this period. The once-grand structure, now in ruins, became a symbol of the mission's decline. Other buildings, such as the adobe living quarters and workshops, also showed signs of wear and neglect, as their new occupants did not prioritize their upkeep.

As the mission buildings fell into disrepair, some were partially occupied, while others were abandoned altogether. The partial occupation often involved makeshift adaptations, with settlers and administrators using the buildings for various ad hoc purposes. This piecemeal approach to occupation further undermined the structural integrity and historical value of the mission complex.

Many indigenous inhabitants, who had relied on the mission for shelter and support, found themselves displaced. Some continued to live in the vicinity of the mission, occupying deteriorating buildings or constructing makeshift shelters. The lack of formal ownership and the precarious living conditions contributed to their ongoing marginalization.

The secularization process also disrupted the agricultural and economic activities that had been central to the mission's self-sufficiency. The mission's fields, orchards, and vineyards, which had been meticulously managed under the mission system, were often neglected or repurposed by their new owners. The fragmentation of land ownership and the decline in coordinated agricultural practices led to a decrease in productivity.

Some of the mission lands were converted into private ranchos, where the new landowners focused on livestock ranching or commercial agriculture. However, the lack of the mission's centralized management and labor force resulted in less efficient land use and reduced output. The economic contributions of the mission buildings and lands diminished significantly during this period of transition.

The secularization of Mission San Juan Capistrano also resulted in a neglect of its cultural and historical significance. The mission buildings, which had been architectural and cultural landmarks, were often viewed primarily as economic assets by the new secular authorities. This utilitarian perspective led to a disregard for the preservation of the mission's historical and cultural heritage.

The artistic and architectural elements that had made the mission unique were often overlooked or damaged during the process of adaptation to new uses. Decorative features, religious artifacts, and architectural details were lost or destroyed, further eroding the mission's cultural legacy.

Despite the widespread neglect and repurposing of the mission buildings, there were individuals and groups within the community who recognized the historical and cultural importance of Mission San Juan Capistrano. These early preservationists sought to protect and maintain the mission buildings, advocating for their restoration and appropriate use.

Local residents, historians, and former mission inhabitants played a crucial role in raising awareness about the mission's deteriorating condition. Their efforts laid the groundwork for future preservation initiatives and highlighted the need to balance economic development with the preservation of cultural heritage.

The changes in ownership and usage of the mission buildings had long-term consequences for Mission San Juan Capistrano and its legacy. The period of secularization marked a significant departure from the mission's original purpose and function, leading to a decline in its physical condition and cultural significance. However, the mission's historical and architectural value continued to resonate with those who recognized its importance.

The challenges and disruptions faced during secularization underscored the complexities of balancing economic, social, and cultural priorities. The lessons learned during this period would later inform efforts to restore and preserve the mission, ensuring that its legacy could be appreciated by future generations.

The secularization of Mission San Juan Capistrano brought about significant changes in the ownership and usage of its buildings. The transition from ecclesiastical to civil control led to a period of neglect, repurposing, and deterioration, as the mission's properties were divided and adapted to new uses. The impact of these changes was deeply felt by the mission's former inhabitants and the broader community, leading to economic hardship, social dislocation, and cultural erosion.

As we move forward in our exploration of Mission San Juan Capistrano's history, the next chapter will focus on the restoration and preservation efforts that sought to reclaim the mission's historical and cultural heritage. Understanding the changes in ownership and usage during the secularization period provides essential context for appreciating the challenges and achievements of these preservation initiatives.

Chapter 6

Restoration and Preservation

Chapter 6: Restoration and Preservation

Efforts to Restore and Preserve the Mission in the Late 19th and Early 20th Centuries

The decline of Mission San Juan Capistrano following its secularization was marked by neglect, repurposing, and deterioration. However, the late 19th and early 20th centuries saw a growing awareness of the mission's historical and cultural significance, sparking efforts to restore and preserve this iconic site. These restoration efforts were driven by a combination of local pride, historical interest, and the broader cultural movement to preserve America's heritage.

By the late 19th century, the state of Mission San Juan Capistrano had become a matter of concern for local residents and historians. The once-thriving mission was in a state of disrepair, with many of its buildings crumbling and overgrown. The Great Stone Church, in particular, stood as a poignant symbol of the mission's decline, its ruins a stark reminder of the earthquake that had destroyed it in 1812.

The first steps towards restoration were often small and localized, undertaken by individuals who recognized the mission's importance. These early preservationists sought to stabilize the remaining structures and prevent further decay. Their efforts included clearing away overgrown vegetation, repairing roofs, and reinforcing walls to protect the buildings from further damage.

Local communities played a crucial role in the early restoration efforts. Residents of San Juan Capistrano and surrounding areas took a keen interest in preserving their local heritage. Community groups and volunteers organized clean-up efforts, fundraising activities, and awareness campaigns to garner support for the mission's restoration.

One significant development was the establishment of local historical societies dedicated to preserving the mission and its history. These societies brought together historians, residents, and other stakeholders who shared a commitment to restoring the mission. They documented the mission's history, conducted research, and advocated for its preservation at local and state levels.

The arts and literature also played a pivotal role in raising awareness about Mission San Juan Capistrano and its plight. The mission's romantic and picturesque ruins captured the imagination of artists, writers, and photographers. Their works helped to popularize the mission and highlight its historical significance.

Notable artists created paintings and drawings of the mission, which were exhibited in galleries and published in books and magazines. These artworks depicted the mission's beauty and historical charm, drawing attention to its deteriorating condition and the need for preservation. Writers and poets also celebrated the mission in their works, weaving its history and mystique into the broader narrative of California's past.

Religious organizations, particularly the Catholic Church, were instrumental in the early restoration efforts. The mission's religious significance as a historic center of Catholicism in California prompted the Church to take an active interest in its preservation. The Church recognized that restoring the mission was not only about preserving a historical site but also about maintaining a spiritual and cultural heritage.

Local parishes and dioceses organized fundraising campaigns to support the restoration efforts. Catholic schools and community groups held events to raise awareness and generate financial support for the mission's upkeep. These religious organizations collaborated with local historical societies and other stakeholders to pool resources and expertise for the mission's restoration.

The broader preservation movement in the United States, which gained momentum in the late 19th and early 20th centuries, provided an important context for the restoration of Mission San Juan Capistrano. This movement sought to protect and preserve America's historical and cultural landmarks, recognizing their value for future generations.

At the national level, the establishment of organizations such as the National Trust for Historic Preservation and the passage of preservation laws reflected a growing commitment to heritage conservation. These developments influenced local and state efforts to preserve historic sites, including Mission San Juan Capistrano.

Government involvement in the mission's restoration became more pronounced in the early 20th century. State and local authorities began to recognize the mission's historical significance and its potential as a cultural and educational resource. Legislative measures were introduced to protect the mission, allocate funds for its restoration, and support preservation initiatives.

Several major restoration projects were undertaken during this period, aiming to stabilize, repair, and restore the mission's buildings. These projects involved extensive research, planning, and collaboration among various stakeholders, including architects, historians, craftsmen, and community volunteers.

One of the key focuses of these restoration projects was the preservation of the mission church and other primary buildings. Efforts were made to repair and reinforce the structures, using historically accurate materials and techniques. Roofs were repaired or replaced, walls were stabilized, and damaged elements were restored to their original condition.

The restoration of the mission's gardens and grounds was another important aspect of these projects. The mission's historic gardens, which had fallen into neglect, were revived based on historical records and archaeological evidence. Pathways were cleared, plants and trees were replanted, and the mission's courtyards were restored to reflect their historical appearance.

Restoring Mission San Juan Capistrano presented numerous challenges. The deteriorated condition of many buildings required innovative approaches to stabilization and repair. Preservationists had to balance the need to use modern materials and techniques with the desire to maintain historical authenticity.

One of the significant challenges was addressing the structural damage caused by the 1812 earthquake and subsequent neglect. The Great Stone Church, in particular, required careful engineering to stabilize its remaining walls and prevent further collapse. Preservationists employed advanced techniques in masonry conservation and structural reinforcement to ensure the stability of the ruins.

Innovations in historical research and documentation also played a crucial role in the restoration efforts. Detailed historical records, photographs, and drawings were used to guide the restoration work, ensuring that the restored elements were as accurate as possible. Archaeological investigations provided valuable insights into the mission's original layout and construction, informing the restoration projects.

A key component of the restoration efforts was engaging the community and educating the public about the mission's historical significance. Community involvement was essential for building support and sustaining the restoration initiatives. Educational programs, tours, and events were organized to raise awareness and foster a sense of ownership and pride among local residents.

Schools and educational institutions played a vital role in this process. Students participated in field trips to the mission, where they learned about its history and the importance of preservation. Educational materials and programs were developed to integrate the mission's history into the broader curriculum, helping to instill a sense of historical consciousness and appreciation among younger generations.

The restoration efforts in the late 19th and early 20th centuries laid the groundwork for a long-term vision of preservation and sustainability for Mission San Juan Capistrano. The goal was not only to restore the mission to its former glory but also to ensure its continued relevance and accessibility for future generations.

This vision included establishing the mission as a historical landmark and cultural center, where visitors could learn about California's mission heritage and the broader history of the region. Plans were made to create interpretive displays, museums, and educational programs that would enhance the visitor experience and provide deeper insights into the mission's historical context.

Sustainability was a key consideration in these efforts. Preservationists recognized the need to maintain the mission buildings and grounds in a way that would ensure their long-term survival. This involved ongoing maintenance, periodic assessments, and adaptive reuse strategies that respected the mission's historical integrity while allowing for contemporary use.

The efforts to restore and preserve Mission San Juan Capistrano in the late 19th and early 20th centuries were marked by a combination of local initiative, community engagement, and broader cultural movements. These efforts helped to save the mission from further decline and laid the foundation for its future as a cherished historical landmark.

As we move forward in our exploration of Mission San Juan Capistrano's history, the next sections will focus on the important figures and organizations involved in the restoration efforts and the mission's establishment as a historical landmark and tourist destination. Understanding the early restoration efforts provides essential context for appreciating the ongoing commitment to preserving this iconic site and its enduring legacy.

Important Figures and Organizations Involved in the Restoration

The restoration and preservation of Mission San Juan Capistrano were driven by the dedication and vision of several key figures and organizations. These individuals and groups recognized the historical and cultural significance of the mission and worked tirelessly to protect and restore it. Their efforts were instrumental in reversing the mission's decline and ensuring its survival for future generations.

One of the most pivotal figures in the restoration of Mission San Juan Capistrano was Father John O'Sullivan. Arriving at the mission in 1910, Father O'Sullivan was deeply moved by the state of disrepair and neglect he encountered. Recognizing the mission's historical and cultural importance, he made it his life's work to restore and preserve the site.

Father O'Sullivan's approach to restoration was hands-on and holistic. He personally supervised the repair and restoration of the mission buildings, often involving local residents and volunteers in the work. Under his leadership, the mission church, which had suffered significant damage, was restored and reopened for worship. His efforts extended beyond the physical restoration to include the revitalization of the mission's gardens and grounds, bringing new life to the historic site.

In addition to his restoration work, Father O'Sullivan was a passionate advocate for the mission's history and legacy. He wrote extensively about the mission, producing books and articles that highlighted its significance and called for broader preservation efforts. His writings helped to raise awareness and garner support for the mission's restoration from both the local community and a wider audience.

The Landmarks Club of Southern California, founded in 1895, played a crucial role in the early preservation efforts of California's missions, including San Juan Capistrano. The club was established by Charles Fletcher Lummis, a journalist, historian, and advocate for the preservation of the Southwest's cultural heritage. Lummis recognized the urgent need to protect the missions from further deterioration and rallied support for their restoration.

The Landmarks Club focused on raising funds and mobilizing resources to repair and stabilize the mission buildings. Their efforts included organizing fundraising campaigns, public lectures, and educational programs to generate awareness and financial support. The club's work provided much-needed resources and expertise, enabling significant progress in the preservation of Mission San Juan Capistrano.

The Native Sons of the Golden West (NSGW), a fraternal organization dedicated to preserving California's history, was another important supporter of the mission's restoration. Founded in 1875, the NSGW was committed to protecting and promoting the state's cultural heritage, including its historic missions.

The NSGW provided financial assistance and advocacy for the restoration of Mission San Juan Capistrano. The organization sponsored restoration projects, funded repairs, and contributed to the maintenance of the mission buildings. Their involvement helped to sustain the momentum of the preservation efforts and ensured that the mission remained a priority for the local and state community.

The Daughters of the American Revolution (DAR), a lineage-based organization focused on historical preservation and education, also played a role in the mission's restoration. The DAR's commitment to preserving American history extended to the Spanish missions, which they recognized as integral to the nation's cultural heritage.

The DAR supported the restoration of Mission San Juan Capistrano through fundraising efforts, volunteer work, and advocacy. Members of the organization participated in restoration projects, helped to document the mission's history, and promoted its significance to a wider audience. Their efforts contributed to the mission's preservation and the broader awareness of its historical value.

The restoration of Mission San Juan Capistrano benefited from the expertise of architects and historians who specialized in historic preservation. These professionals brought technical knowledge and historical insight to the restoration projects, ensuring that the work was both accurate and respectful of the mission's heritage.

Notable architects, such as Arthur B. Benton, were involved in the restoration efforts. Benton, a prominent advocate for the preservation of California's missions, provided architectural guidance and design expertise. His work included detailed plans for restoring the mission buildings and ensuring their structural stability while maintaining historical authenticity.

Historians played a crucial role in researching and documenting the mission's history, providing the context and background necessary for informed restoration. Their scholarship helped to guide the restoration efforts and ensure that the work was grounded in a thorough understanding of the mission's past.

Local community organizations and civic groups were instrumental in the restoration and preservation of Mission San Juan Capistrano. These groups, composed of residents, business owners, and civic leaders, recognized the mission's importance to their community and worked together to support its restoration.

One such organization was the San Juan Capistrano Historical Society, which was established to promote the preservation and appreciation of the town's historical sites, including the mission. The society organized events, fundraisers, and educational programs to support the mission's restoration and engage the local community in its preservation.

Government support at the local, state, and federal levels was crucial in the restoration efforts. Recognition of the mission's historical significance led to legislative measures and funding allocations aimed at its preservation. State and local governments provided grants and resources to support restoration projects and maintenance.

The mission's designation as a historical landmark facilitated access to additional resources and protections. This official recognition helped to ensure that the mission's restoration was a priority and that it received the necessary support to continue its preservation efforts.

The restoration and preservation of Mission San Juan Capistrano were characterized by collaborative efforts and a long-term commitment from various stakeholders. The combined efforts of religious leaders, preservation organizations, community groups, architects, historians, and government entities created a robust framework for the mission's restoration.

These collaborative efforts were essential in overcoming the challenges of restoration, including funding shortages, technical difficulties, and the need for historical accuracy. The shared commitment to preserving the mission's heritage fostered a sense of unity and purpose, ensuring that the restoration work was sustained over time.

The restoration and preservation of Mission San Juan Capistrano were made possible through the dedication and efforts of numerous important figures and organizations. From the visionary leadership of Father John O'Sullivan to the advocacy and support of groups like the Landmarks Club, the Native Sons of the Golden West, and the Daughters of the American Revolution, these efforts laid the foundation for the mission's continued preservation.

The involvement of architects, historians, and local community organizations further ensured that the restoration work was carried out with care and respect for the mission's historical and cultural significance. Government support and legislation provided the necessary resources and protections to sustain these efforts.

As we continue our exploration of Mission San Juan Capistrano's history, the next section will focus on the mission's establishment as a historical landmark and tourist destination. Understanding the contributions of the key figures and organizations involved in the restoration provides essential context for appreciating the mission's enduring legacy and its role as a cherished cultural treasure.

The Mission as a Historical Landmark and Tourist Destination

The restoration and preservation efforts at Mission San Juan Capistrano during the late 19th and early 20th centuries laid the groundwork for its transformation into a celebrated historical landmark and popular tourist destination. This transformation was driven by a combination of historical significance, cultural appeal, and dedicated efforts to promote and maintain the site as a place of public interest and education.

The formal recognition of Mission San Juan Capistrano as a historical landmark was a critical step in its preservation journey. Official landmark status provided legal protections and helped secure funding for ongoing restoration and maintenance efforts. In 1933, the mission was designated a California Historical Landmark, which highlighted its importance to the state's heritage and ensured its protection under state preservation laws.

Further recognition came in 1971 when Mission San Juan Capistrano was added to the National Register of Historic Places. This federal designation underscored the mission's significance at the national level and facilitated access to additional resources and support for preservation. The inclusion in the National Register also helped raise awareness about the mission's historical and cultural value, attracting more visitors and scholars.

The transformation of Mission San Juan Capistrano into a tourist destination required the development of infrastructure to accommodate and enhance the visitor experience. This development included the construction of visitor centers, museums, and interpretive displays that provided context and information about the mission's history.

A key component of this infrastructure was the establishment of guided tours and educational programs. Trained docents and guides led visitors through the mission complex, offering insights into its history, architecture, and cultural significance. These tours helped bring the mission's past to life, allowing visitors to engage with the site in a meaningful and educational way.

The creation of museums and exhibit spaces within the mission complex further enriched the visitor experience. These spaces showcased artifacts, documents, and artworks related to the mission's history, providing a tangible connection to the past. Exhibits were designed to be informative and engaging, catering to diverse audiences, including school groups, families, and history enthusiasts.

Cultural and educational programs became central to the mission's role as a historical landmark. These programs aimed to educate the public about the mission's history and significance, as well as to celebrate the cultural heritage of the indigenous peoples and the Spanish colonial period.

Educational initiatives included school field trips, workshops, and special events tailored to different age groups and interests. Schools from across California brought students to the mission to learn about its history firsthand. These field trips often included interactive activities, such as reenactments, crafts, and storytelling, which made history accessible and engaging for young learners.

Cultural programs, such as music and dance performances, art exhibits, and festivals, celebrated the mission's diverse heritage. These events highlighted the contributions of the indigenous Acjachemen people, the Spanish missionaries, and the broader community. They provided a platform for cultural expression and appreciation, fostering a deeper understanding of the mission's historical context.

The promotion and marketing of Mission San Juan Capistrano as a tourist destination played a crucial role in attracting visitors and sustaining interest in the site. Efforts to promote the mission included advertising campaigns, partnerships with travel and tourism organizations, and the use of media to highlight its attractions.

Brochures, posters, and advertisements showcased the mission's unique features, such as the beautiful gardens, the iconic bell tower, and the historic church. These promotional materials were distributed through various channels, including visitor centers, hotels, and travel agencies, reaching a wide audience.

The mission's association with the annual return of the swallows, a natural event that captures the public's imagination, became a focal point for marketing efforts. The swallows' migration to San Juan Capistrano each spring drew significant media attention and brought thousands of visitors to the mission. This phenomenon was celebrated with the annual Swallows Day Parade and related festivities, further enhancing the mission's appeal as a tourist destination.

Events and festivals at Mission San Juan Capistrano played a significant role in attracting visitors and fostering a sense of community. These events ranged from historical reenactments and cultural celebrations to religious observances and community gatherings. They provided opportunities for visitors to experience the mission's history and culture in an interactive and engaging way.

One of the most notable events was the annual Swallows Day Parade, which celebrated the return of the swallows to San Juan Capistrano each spring. The parade and associated festivities, including music, dancing, and crafts, drew large crowds and highlighted the mission's connection to natural and cultural heritage. This event became a beloved tradition and a major attraction for both locals and tourists.

Other events included historical reenactments, which brought the mission's past to life through dramatizations of significant moments in its history. These reenactments involved participants dressed in period costumes, engaging in activities such as colonial-era crafts, traditional dances, and religious ceremonies. These events provided an immersive experience for visitors, allowing them to step back in time and gain a deeper understanding of the mission's history.

The concept of living history played a central role in the preservation and presentation of Mission San Juan Capistrano. Rather than being treated solely as a static historical artifact, the mission was envisioned as a living history site where the past could be experienced in a dynamic and interactive manner.

Living history programs involved recreating aspects of daily life at the mission during its peak years. These programs included demonstrations of traditional crafts, agricultural practices, and cooking methods, allowing visitors to witness and participate in activities that were integral to mission life. The involvement of costumed interpreters and artisans added authenticity to these experiences, making history tangible and relatable.

The living history approach also emphasized the ongoing relevance of the mission's heritage. By connecting the past with the present, these programs highlighted the mission's enduring cultural significance and its role as a vibrant part of the community.

A crucial aspect of the mission's transformation into a historical landmark was the collaboration with indigenous communities, particularly the Acjachemen people. Recognizing the importance of honoring and preserving indigenous heritage, the mission worked closely with Acjachemen representatives to ensure that their history and contributions were accurately and respectfully represented.

Collaborative efforts included the inclusion of indigenous perspectives in interpretive displays and educational programs. Indigenous artisans and cultural practitioners were invited to participate in events and workshops, sharing their knowledge and traditions with visitors. These collaborations helped to create a more inclusive and comprehensive narrative of the mission's history.

The mission also supported efforts to revitalize and preserve indigenous languages, crafts, and traditions. Language classes, cultural workshops, and heritage events provided opportunities for the Acjachemen community to connect with their cultural roots and share their heritage with a broader audience.

Enhancing the visitor experience and engagement was a key focus of the mission's development as a tourist destination. Efforts were made to create a welcoming and informative environment that catered to the diverse interests and needs of visitors.

Interactive exhibits, multimedia presentations, and hands-on activities were incorporated into the mission's offerings to provide a more engaging and educational experience. These elements allowed visitors to explore the mission's history through various sensory modalities, making learning more accessible and enjoyable.

Visitor feedback and input were also valued and used to continually improve the mission's programs and facilities. Surveys, suggestion boxes, and focus groups provided insights into visitor preferences and helped guide the development of new initiatives and improvements.

The transformation of Mission San Juan Capistrano into a historical landmark and tourist destination had significant economic and social impacts on the local community. The influx of visitors contributed to the local economy, supporting businesses such as hotels, restaurants, shops, and tour services. The mission became a key driver of tourism, attracting visitors from across the country and around the world.

Socially, the mission's preservation and promotion fostered a sense of pride and identity among local residents. The mission's history and heritage became central to the community's cultural narrative, providing a shared sense of connection to the past. Community involvement in the mission's events and programs further strengthened these bonds and encouraged a collective commitment to preservation.

The efforts to restore and preserve Mission San Juan Capistrano in the late 19th and early 20th centuries successfully transformed it into a celebrated historical landmark and popular tourist destination. Through official recognition, development of visitor infrastructure, cultural and educational programs, and collaborative efforts, the mission became a place where history is preserved, celebrated, and experienced.

The mission's journey from neglect and decline to restoration and prominence reflects the dedication of those who recognized its value and worked tirelessly to protect and promote it. As a living history site, the mission continues to educate and inspire visitors, serving as a testament to the rich cultural heritage of California and the enduring legacy of its missions.

As we move forward to the next chapter, we will explore the current state of Mission San Juan Capistrano, examining its ongoing preservation efforts, community engagement, and role as a cultural and educational resource in the present day. Understanding the mission's transformation into a historical landmark provides essential context for appreciating its significance and continued relevance.

The Mission's Role in the Local Community and Its Educational Programs

Mission San Juan Capistrano today serves as a vibrant center for education, culture, and community engagement. Its role in the local community extends beyond its historical significance, making it an integral part of the cultural and educational landscape of Southern California. The mission's diverse educational programs and community initiatives highlight its continued relevance and its commitment to preserving and sharing its rich heritage.

Mission San Juan Capistrano has developed a comprehensive array of educational programs designed to cater to various age groups and interests. These programs aim to provide in-depth knowledge about the mission's history, architecture, and cultural impact, as well as to foster an appreciation for the broader history of California.

One of the cornerstone educational initiatives at the mission is its robust field trip program. Schools from across California and beyond bring students to the mission to experience history firsthand. These field trips are tailored to different grade levels, ensuring that the content is age-appropriate and engaging.

Students participate in guided tours that cover the mission's history, from its founding by Father Junípero Serra to its role in the Spanish colonial period and its transformation over the centuries. These tours often include interactive elements, such as hands-on activities and demonstrations of traditional crafts and trades, which help students connect with the past in a tangible way.

To enhance the educational impact, the mission provides teachers with curriculum guides and lesson plans that align with state educational standards. These resources are designed to integrate the mission's history into the broader social studies curriculum, covering topics such as California history, Native American cultures, and the Spanish colonial era. The curriculum materials include pre-visit activities, in-mission assignments, and post-visit projects, creating a comprehensive educational experience.

In addition to school programs, Mission San Juan Capistrano offers summer camps and workshops that provide more immersive educational experiences. These programs are designed to engage children and teens in learning through interactive activities, creative projects, and historical reenactments. Participants might learn how to make adobe bricks, weave traditional baskets, or perform in a play about the mission's history.

Summer camps often focus on specific themes, such as archaeology, art, or ecology, allowing participants to explore different aspects of the mission's heritage. These programs help to foster a love of history and a deeper understanding of the mission's role in the region's development.

The mission also caters to adult learners through a variety of educational programs and lecture series. These programs feature experts in history, archaeology, architecture, and cultural studies who provide in-depth insights into different facets of the mission's past and its ongoing preservation.

Lectures and seminars cover a wide range of topics, from the architectural techniques used in the mission's construction to the daily lives of the indigenous Acjachemen people. These events attract a diverse audience, including local residents, historians, and tourists, and contribute to the ongoing dialogue about the mission's significance and legacy.

To enhance the educational experience, Mission San Juan Capistrano hosts special exhibits and interactive displays that delve into specific aspects of its history. These exhibits are often curated in collaboration with historians, archaeologists, and cultural institutions, ensuring accuracy and depth.

Interactive displays use modern technology to engage visitors in innovative ways. For example, digital kiosks might allow visitors to explore detailed maps of the mission grounds, view historical photographs, or watch videos about restoration efforts. Augmented reality (AR) experiences can bring history to life by overlaying historical images and information onto the mission's physical landscape, providing a dynamic and immersive learning experience.

The mission's role in the local community extends beyond its educational programs. It actively engages with residents through a variety of outreach initiatives that promote cultural awareness, historical preservation, and community involvement.

Volunteers play a crucial role in the mission's operations and community outreach. The mission's volunteer program offers opportunities for individuals to contribute their time and skills in areas such as guiding tours, assisting with events, and participating in restoration projects. Volunteers are often local residents who are passionate about history and committed to preserving their community's heritage.

The mission also collaborates with local schools, universities, and community organizations to involve students and young adults in volunteer activities. These partnerships provide valuable hands-on experience and foster a sense of stewardship and civic responsibility among younger generations.

Mission San Juan Capistrano partners with various cultural and historical organizations to promote the preservation and celebration of the region's heritage. These partnerships include collaborations with indigenous groups, historical societies, and cultural institutions, which help to ensure that the mission's programs and exhibits reflect diverse perspectives and historical accuracy.

The mission works closely with the Acjachemen community to honor their cultural heritage and incorporate their history into the mission's narrative. This collaboration includes joint events, cultural demonstrations, and educational programs that highlight the contributions and experiences of the indigenous people who lived at the mission.

Public events and celebrations are a key aspect of the mission's community engagement. These events provide opportunities for residents and visitors to come together and celebrate the mission's heritage in a festive and inclusive environment.

The mission hosts a variety of public events throughout the year, including historical reenactments, cultural festivals, and holiday celebrations. These events often feature music, dance, food, and crafts that reflect the diverse cultural influences of the mission's history. Community participation in these events fosters a sense of pride and connection to the mission's legacy.

To promote historical preservation, the mission offers programs that educate the community about the importance of preserving cultural heritage. Workshops and seminars on topics such as historic preservation techniques, genealogy, and local history provide residents with the knowledge and tools to contribute to preservation efforts.

The mission also engages in advocacy and fundraising to support ongoing restoration and preservation projects. Community involvement in these initiatives is encouraged through membership programs, donation drives, and special campaigns that highlight specific restoration needs and goals.

As a major tourist destination, Mission San Juan Capistrano plays a significant role in the local economy. The influx of visitors supports local businesses, including hotels, restaurants, and shops, and contributes to the overall economic vitality of the region.

The mission's status as a historical landmark attracts tourists from across the country and around the world, making it a key driver of tourism in Southern California. Marketing efforts and partnerships with travel and tourism organizations help to promote the mission as a must-visit destination, enhancing its visibility and appeal.

Mission San Juan Capistrano today stands as a beacon of historical and cultural education, deeply embedded in the fabric of the local community. Its diverse educational programs, from school field trips and summer camps to adult lectures and interactive exhibits, provide valuable learning opportunities for people of all ages. The mission's outreach initiatives and community partnerships ensure that it remains a vibrant and inclusive center for cultural engagement and historical preservation.

By actively involving the community in its programs and events, the mission fosters a sense of shared heritage and civic pride. Its impact on the local economy and tourism further underscores its significance as a cultural and economic asset. As we continue our exploration of Mission San Juan Capistrano's present-day role, the next sections will delve into its annual events and cultural celebrations, as well as its continuing legacy and significance in California's history.

Annual Events and Cultural Celebrations, Such as the Swallows' Day Parade

Mission San Juan Capistrano is not only a historical landmark but also a vibrant cultural hub that hosts a variety of annual events and cultural celebrations. These events play a crucial role in bringing the community together, celebrating the mission's rich heritage, and attracting visitors from near and far. Among these, the Swallows' Day Parade stands out as a signature event, but there are many other celebrations that contribute to the mission's dynamic cultural calendar.

The Swallows' Day Parade is perhaps the most iconic event associated with Mission San Juan Capistrano. Celebrated annually in March, this parade commemorates the legendary return of the swallows to the mission, a natural phenomenon that has captivated the public's imagination for generations.

The legend of the swallows' return dates back to the early 20th century when Father John O'Sullivan, one of the mission's key restorers, noticed the birds nesting in the ruins of the Great Stone Church. The annual return of the swallows to San Juan Capistrano, typically around St. Joseph's Day (March 19), became a symbol of renewal and continuity, linking the present to the mission's storied past.

The Swallows' Day Parade celebrates this natural event and has grown into one of the largest non-motorized parades in the United States. The parade features a colorful procession of floats, marching bands, equestrian units, dancers, and community groups, all celebrating the return of the swallows and the cultural heritage of San Juan Capistrano.

Community involvement is a hallmark of the Swallows' Day Parade. Local schools, civic organizations, businesses, and cultural groups participate in the parade, showcasing their creativity and community spirit. The event is organized by the San Juan Capistrano Fiesta Association, a nonprofit organization dedicated to preserving and promoting the cultural traditions of the area.

The parade is just one part of the larger Swallows' Day celebration, which includes a week of festivities leading up to the parade. These festivities often feature a variety of events such as the Fiesta de las Golondrinas (Festival of the Swallows), which includes live music, traditional dance performances, food stalls, and arts and crafts vendors. The celebration provides a festive atmosphere that attracts thousands of visitors and fosters a strong sense of community pride.

While the Swallows' Day Parade is the most famous, Mission San Juan Capistrano hosts numerous other annual events and cultural celebrations that highlight its historical and cultural significance.

In addition to the Swallows' Day Parade, the mission hosts a special celebration on St. Joseph's Day, March 19, marking the traditional date of the swallows' return. This celebration includes a range of activities such as special Mass services, bell ringing, educational programs, and bird-watching tours. The event emphasizes the mission's connection to natural cycles and its role as a sanctuary for wildlife.

Christmas at the Mission is a cherished annual event that transforms the mission into a festive wonderland. The celebration features a variety of holiday-themed activities, including carol singing, nativity scenes, live music, and a Christmas tree lighting ceremony. Visitors can explore the mission grounds adorned with festive decorations, enjoy hot cocoa and seasonal treats, and participate in holiday crafts and activities. This event brings the community together to celebrate the holiday season in a historic and picturesque setting.

MissionFest is an annual event that celebrates the mission's cultural heritage with a focus on food, music, and community. This festival features live performances by local and regional musicians, showcasing a variety of genres from classical to contemporary. Food vendors offer a diverse array of culinary delights, reflecting the multicultural influences of the region. MissionFest also includes art exhibits, craft booths, and activities for children, making it a family-friendly event that attracts visitors of all ages.

The mission regularly hosts historical reenactments and living history days, where visitors can experience what life was like during the mission era. These events often feature costumed interpreters who demonstrate traditional crafts, cooking methods, agricultural practices, and daily routines of the 18th and 19th centuries. Visitors can participate in hands-on activities, such as making adobe bricks, weaving baskets, and grinding corn, providing an immersive educational experience.

The California Missions Conference is an annual event hosted by Mission San Juan Capistrano that brings together historians, archaeologists, preservationists, and educators to discuss topics related to the California missions. The conference includes lectures, panel discussions, workshops, and field trips to other historic sites. It provides a platform for sharing research, best practices, and new discoveries, contributing to the ongoing scholarship and preservation of California's mission heritage.

The mission also hosts a variety of cultural festivals and international events that celebrate the diverse heritage of the region. These festivals often highlight the traditions of different cultural groups, including Native American, Mexican, Spanish, and other communities that have influenced the mission's history. Events such as Dia de los Muertos (Day of the Dead), Cinco de Mayo, and the Acjachemen Cultural Festival offer opportunities for cultural exchange and celebration, fostering a greater understanding and appreciation of the mission's multicultural legacy.

Throughout the year, the mission offers themed tours that focus on specific aspects of its history and heritage. These tours are often tied to annual events and celebrations, providing visitors with deeper insights into the mission's past. Themes might include the architecture of the mission, the lives of the indigenous Acjachemen people, the role of the mission in the Spanish colonial period, and the natural history of the area.

Workshops and craft fairs are also regular features of the mission's annual calendar. These events offer visitors the chance to learn traditional crafts and skills, such as pottery, weaving, blacksmithing, and candle making. Craft fairs provide a platform for local artisans to showcase and sell their handmade goods, promoting the preservation of traditional crafts and supporting the local economy.

The mission's beautiful and historic setting makes it a perfect venue for concerts and performances. Throughout the year, the mission hosts a variety of musical and theatrical events, ranging from classical music concerts to contemporary performances. These events take advantage of the mission's unique acoustics and atmosphere, offering audiences a memorable cultural experience.

Family Days and children's programs are designed to engage younger visitors with the mission's history and heritage. These events often include storytelling sessions, interactive games, scavenger hunts, and craft activities. Family Days provide an opportunity for parents and children to explore the mission together and learn about its significance in a fun and accessible way.

Mission San Juan Capistrano frequently collaborates with local and regional organizations to enhance its annual events and cultural celebrations. Partnerships with schools, universities, cultural institutions, and community groups help to enrich the mission's programs and extend its reach. These collaborations ensure that the mission remains a vital part of the cultural fabric of Southern California.

The annual events and cultural celebrations at Mission San Juan Capistrano play a crucial role in preserving and promoting the mission's rich heritage. From the iconic Swallows' Day Parade to a wide array of festivals, reenactments, workshops, and performances, these events engage the community and attract visitors from around the world. They highlight the mission's historical significance, celebrate its multicultural legacy, and foster a sense of community pride and connection.

As we continue our exploration of Mission San Juan Capistrano's present-day role, the next section will delve into the mission's continuing legacy and its significance in California's history. Understanding the mission's annual events and cultural celebrations provides essential context for appreciating its ongoing impact and relevance.

The Mission's Continuing Legacy and Its Significance in California's History

Mission San Juan Capistrano's continuing legacy and its significance in California's history are deeply rooted in its multifaceted role as a historical landmark, cultural center, and educational resource. The mission stands as a testament to the enduring impact of the California mission system, reflecting the complex interplay of indigenous, Spanish, and Mexican influences that have shaped the state's development. Today, Mission San Juan Capistrano not only preserves this rich heritage but also serves as a dynamic institution that fosters cultural understanding, historical awareness, and community engagement.

Mission San Juan Capistrano's legacy is intrinsically linked to its role in preserving cultural heritage. The mission's structures, artifacts, and landscapes provide a tangible connection to California's past, allowing visitors to experience the history and culture of the region firsthand. Through meticulous restoration efforts and ongoing maintenance, the mission has retained its architectural integrity and historical authenticity, offering a window into the lives of those who lived and worked there over the centuries.

The preservation of the mission extends beyond its physical structures. The mission actively works to protect and celebrate the cultural traditions of the indigenous Acjachemen people, whose ancestors built and sustained the mission. Collaborative efforts with the Acjachemen community ensure that their history and contributions are recognized and honored, fostering a deeper appreciation for the diverse cultural influences that have shaped the mission's history.

The educational impact of Mission San Juan Capistrano is a cornerstone of its continuing legacy. The mission's comprehensive educational programs provide valuable learning opportunities for students, educators, researchers, and the general public. By offering a wide range of educational activities, from school field trips and workshops to lectures and special exhibits, the mission helps to cultivate a deeper understanding of California's history and heritage.

Mission San Juan Capistrano also serves as an important center for historical scholarship. Researchers and historians use the mission's archives, artifacts, and resources to conduct studies that contribute to the broader understanding of the California mission system and its impact. These scholarly endeavors not only enhance the mission's own programs but also inform the wider historical discourse, shedding light on the complexities of California's colonial past.

As a cultural center, Mission San Juan Capistrano plays a vital role in fostering cultural exchange and community engagement. The mission's diverse array of cultural events and celebrations, including the iconic Swallows' Day Parade, Dia de los Muertos festivities, and traditional music and dance performances, provide platforms for different cultural expressions. These events celebrate the mission's multicultural heritage and promote a sense of unity and inclusivity within the community.

The mission's community engagement initiatives extend to partnerships with local organizations, schools, and cultural groups. These collaborations enhance the mission's programs and ensure that they are accessible and relevant to a broad audience. By actively involving the community in its activities, the mission strengthens its role as a shared cultural and historical resource, fostering a collective sense of ownership and pride.

Mission San Juan Capistrano's significance in California's history is also reflected in its economic and social contributions. As a major tourist destination, the mission attracts visitors from around the world, contributing to the local and regional economy. The influx of tourists supports local businesses, including hotels, restaurants, and shops, and creates jobs within the community.

The mission's events and programs also generate economic activity by drawing large crowds and encouraging spending on services and goods. The economic benefits of the mission extend beyond direct tourism revenue, as the presence of a well-preserved historical site enhances the overall attractiveness of the region as a place to live, work, and visit.

Socially, the mission provides a gathering place for community members to come together and celebrate their shared heritage. The mission's inclusive approach to programming ensures that people from diverse backgrounds feel welcome and valued. This social cohesion contributes to the overall well-being of the community and reinforces the mission's role as a cornerstone of local identity and pride.

The history of Mission San Juan Capistrano is a testament to resilience and adaptation. The mission has withstood natural disasters, political upheavals, and periods of neglect, emerging each time with renewed purpose and vitality. This resilience is a defining characteristic of the mission's legacy, symbolizing the enduring spirit of the people who have contributed to its preservation and revitalization.

The mission's ability to adapt to changing circumstances and needs is also a key aspect of its continuing significance. From its origins as a Spanish colonial mission to its current role as a historical landmark and cultural center, Mission San Juan Capistrano has continuously evolved to meet the challenges and opportunities of each era. This adaptability ensures that the mission remains relevant and meaningful to contemporary audiences while honoring its historical roots.

Mission San Juan Capistrano's legacy serves as an inspiration for future generations. The mission's commitment to preservation, education, and cultural celebration provides a model for other historical sites and institutions. By demonstrating the value of protecting and promoting cultural heritage, the mission encourages others to engage in similar efforts within their own communities.

The mission's educational programs, in particular, play a crucial role in inspiring young people to take an active interest in history and heritage. By providing immersive and engaging learning experiences, the mission fosters a sense of curiosity and appreciation for the past. This educational impact extends beyond the immediate experience, influencing how young people perceive and value history throughout their lives.

Mission San Juan Capistrano's significance extends beyond California, earning national and international recognition for its historical and cultural contributions. The mission's inclusion in the National Register of Historic

Places and its designation as a California Historical Landmark underscore its importance as a site of national heritage. These recognitions highlight the mission's role in the broader narrative of American history and its contributions to the cultural tapestry of the United States.

Internationally, the mission is recognized as a symbol of the Spanish colonial era and the cultural exchanges that occurred between Europe and the Americas. Visitors from around the world come to San Juan Capistrano to experience its history and architecture, contributing to a global appreciation of the mission's significance. This international recognition reinforces the mission's status as a cultural and historical treasure with a lasting impact.

Mission San Juan Capistrano's continuing legacy and significance in California's history are multifaceted and profound. As a preserved historical landmark, the mission offers a tangible connection to the past, allowing visitors to explore the rich heritage of the region. Its comprehensive educational programs, cultural events, and community engagement initiatives ensure that this heritage is actively shared and celebrated.

The mission's economic and social contributions highlight its role as a vital part of the local and regional community, while its resilience and adaptability serve as a symbol of enduring strength and relevance. By inspiring future generations and earning national and international recognition, Mission San Juan Capistrano continues to play a pivotal role in preserving and promoting California's cultural heritage.

As we move forward in our exploration of Mission San Juan Capistrano, the next chapter will provide a recap of the mission's historical importance and encourage readers to visit the mission and continue learning about its history. Understanding the mission's continuing legacy and significance provides essential context for appreciating its enduring impact and relevance in today's world.

Conclusion

Conclusion

Mission San Juan Capistrano, often referred to as the "Jewel of the California Missions," holds a unique and significant place in the history of California and the broader narrative of the Spanish colonial era in the Americas. Its historical importance is underscored by its architectural beauty, its role in the cultural and religious transformation of the region, and its enduring legacy as a center of community and cultural preservation.

Founded on November 1, 1776, by Father Junípero Serra, Mission San Juan Capistrano was the seventh of the 21 California missions established by the Spanish Franciscans. Its foundation marked a crucial phase in the Spanish colonization of Alta California, a territory that was then part of the Spanish Empire. The establishment of the mission aimed to convert the local indigenous population, primarily the Acjachemen (Juaneño) people, to Christianity and integrate them into the Spanish colonial system.

The early years of the mission were marked by the construction of essential buildings and the development of agricultural activities. The mission quickly became a thriving center of agriculture, producing crops such as wheat, barley, corn, and vegetables. Livestock farming also flourished, with large herds of cattle, sheep, and horses providing meat, milk, wool, and hides. The introduction of European farming techniques and livestock had a profound impact on the local landscape and economy.

Mission San Juan Capistrano is renowned for its architectural beauty and innovation. The mission complex includes a variety of buildings constructed using traditional Spanish colonial techniques, adapted to local materials and conditions. The adobe and stone structures, with their red-tiled roofs and arched corridors, exemplify the mission style that became iconic in California.

One of the mission's most significant architectural achievements was the construction of the Great Stone Church, which began in 1797. Designed in the shape of a cross and featuring a large nave, side chapels, and a bell tower, the Great Stone Church was an impressive example of mission architecture. Unfortunately, the church was severely damaged by an earthquake in 1812, but its ruins remain a poignant symbol of the mission's historical and cultural legacy.

The establishment of Mission San Juan Capistrano brought about significant cultural and social changes for the indigenous Acjachemen people. The mission system sought to convert the indigenous population to Christianity and transform their way of life according to Spanish customs and practices. This process of cultural transformation included religious instruction, the adoption of European agricultural practices, and the integration of the Acjachemen into the mission's economic activities.

The impact of the mission on the Acjachemen was profound and complex. While the mission provided new opportunities for education and skill development, it also disrupted traditional social structures and ways of life. The forced relocation to the mission, the imposition of new religious practices, and the loss of traditional lands and autonomy had lasting effects on the Acjachemen community. Despite these challenges, the Acjachemen people demonstrated resilience and adaptability, contributing significantly to the mission's operations and cultural heritage.

Throughout its history, Mission San Juan Capistrano was a vital economic and social center in the region. The mission's agricultural and craft production supported not only its own community but also the broader Spanish colonial economy. The mission's fields, orchards, and workshops produced surplus goods that were traded with other missions and settlements, creating a network of economic exchange.

Socially, the mission served as a hub of community life. It provided education, healthcare, and social services to its inhabitants, fostering a sense of community and shared purpose. The mission's religious festivals and communal activities brought people together, reinforcing social bonds and cultural identity. The mission's role as a social and economic center extended beyond its immediate community, influencing the development of the surrounding region.

The period of secularization in the early 19th century marked a significant turning point in the history of Mission San Juan Capistrano. Following Mexico's independence from Spain in 1821, the new Mexican government implemented policies to secularize the missions and redistribute their lands. The secularization process, which began in 1834, aimed to transfer mission properties from ecclesiastical to civil control and integrate the indigenous population into Mexican society.

Secularization brought about a period of decline for Mission San Juan Capistrano. The mission's lands were divided and distributed to settlers, and many of its buildings fell into disrepair. The departure of the Franciscan missionaries and the loss of centralized management led to economic hardship and social dislocation for the mission's inhabitants. Despite these challenges, the mission's historical and cultural significance remained, setting the stage for future preservation efforts.

The late 19th and early 20th centuries saw renewed efforts to restore and preserve Mission San Juan Capistrano. Visionaries like Father John O'Sullivan played a crucial role in stabilizing and restoring the mission's buildings, recognizing the importance of preserving this historical landmark. These restoration efforts were supported by local communities, historical societies, and preservation organizations, who rallied to protect and celebrate the mission's heritage.

The restoration work included repairing the mission church, reinforcing the remaining structures, and revitalizing the mission gardens. These efforts not only preserved the mission's physical integrity but also revived its role as a center of community and cultural activity. The mission's restoration became a symbol of resilience and renewal, highlighting the enduring value of preserving historical sites.

Today, Mission San Juan Capistrano continues to play a vital role in preserving California's cultural heritage. As a historical landmark and popular tourist destination, the mission attracts visitors from around the world, offering them a chance to explore its rich history and architectural beauty. The mission's educational programs, cultural events, and community initiatives ensure that its legacy is actively shared and celebrated.

The mission's ongoing preservation efforts reflect a commitment to maintaining its historical integrity and relevance. By fostering a deeper understanding of the mission's history and its impact on California's development, Mission San Juan Capistrano serves as a bridge between the past and the present. Its significance extends beyond its historical origins, embodying the diverse cultural influences that have shaped California's identity.

Mission San Juan Capistrano's historical importance is multifaceted and profound. From its founding by Father Junípero Serra to its role as a center of economic, social, and cultural activity, the mission has left an indelible mark on California's history. The complex interplay of indigenous, Spanish, and Mexican influences at the mission reflects the broader narrative of cultural exchange and transformation that characterizes the region's development.

The mission's legacy of resilience, adaptation, and renewal continues to inspire preservation efforts and community engagement. As a living history site, Mission San Juan Capistrano offers valuable insights into the past while serving as a vibrant center for cultural celebration and education. Its enduring significance underscores the importance of preserving historical landmarks and honoring the diverse heritage that shapes our collective identity.

Mission San Juan Capistrano stands as a testament to the enduring legacy of California's rich cultural and historical tapestry. Visiting the mission offers a unique opportunity to step back in time and experience the profound influence of the Spanish mission system, the resilience of the indigenous Acjachemen people, and the vibrant history of the region. As you explore the mission, you will find yourself immersed in a world where past and present seamlessly blend, providing invaluable insights into the forces that have shaped California.

There is no substitute for experiencing Mission San Juan Capistrano firsthand. Walking through its storied corridors, standing beneath the arches of its adobe structures, and exploring its beautifully restored gardens provide a tangible connection to the past. Each building, artifact, and landscape feature tells a story of perseverance, cultural exchange, and historical transformation.

Visiting the mission allows you to appreciate the architectural ingenuity of the Great Stone Church, feel the serenity of the mission's chapel, and admire the craftsmanship of the original mission artisans. The mission's preserved spaces offer a glimpse into the daily lives of the people who built, maintained, and lived within its walls. Engaging with the mission in person deepens your understanding and appreciation of its significance.

Mission San Juan Capistrano offers a wealth of educational programs designed to enhance your visit and provide deeper insights into its history. Whether you are a student, educator, history enthusiast, or casual visitor, these programs cater to diverse interests and learning levels. Guided tours, led by knowledgeable docents, provide detailed narratives of the mission's history, architecture, and cultural impact.

The mission's educational initiatives also include interactive exhibits, hands-on workshops, and thematic tours that explore specific aspects of its heritage. Participating in these programs enriches your experience and offers a comprehensive understanding of the mission's multifaceted history. The educational resources available at the mission make it a dynamic learning environment for visitors of all ages.

Attending one of the mission's annual cultural celebrations or events offers an engaging way to connect with its living history. The Swallows' Day Parade, Christmas at the Mission, Dia de los Muertos celebrations, and other events provide vibrant, interactive experiences that celebrate the mission's cultural legacy. These events showcase traditional music, dance, crafts, and cuisine, offering a festive and immersive way to learn about the mission's historical and contemporary significance.

Participating in these celebrations not only enriches your understanding of the mission but also connects you with the local community and its traditions. These events highlight the mission's role as a cultural hub and demonstrate how its legacy continues to thrive in modern times. By engaging with the mission's cultural events, you become part of a broader effort to preserve and celebrate California's diverse heritage.

Your visit to Mission San Juan Capistrano also contributes to ongoing preservation efforts. The mission relies on the support of visitors, members, and donors to maintain its historical structures and programs. By visiting the mission, you help fund essential restoration and conservation projects that ensure its longevity for future generations.

Consider becoming a member of the mission or contributing to its preservation initiatives. Membership provides benefits such as free admission, special event invitations, and access to exclusive programs. Your support helps sustain the mission's educational and cultural activities, allowing it to continue serving as a vital historical and community resource.

Mission San Juan Capistrano is part of a larger network of California missions, each with its own unique history and contributions to the state's development. Visiting other missions in the region offers a broader perspective on the mission system and its impact. Each mission provides different insights into the historical, architectural, and cultural dimensions of this significant era.

By exploring multiple missions, you can appreciate the diversity and commonalities among them, deepening your understanding of the Spanish colonial period in California. The interconnected stories of the missions create a richer, more nuanced picture of the past, highlighting the complex interactions between indigenous populations, Spanish colonizers, and later Mexican and American influences.

Your visit to Mission San Juan Capistrano is just the beginning of a lifelong journey of learning and discovery. The mission's history offers countless avenues for further exploration, whether through books, documentaries, academic research, or discussions with historians and cultural experts. The mission's gift shop provides resources such as historical texts, scholarly publications, and educational materials that can enhance your knowledge.

Sharing your experiences and knowledge with others helps to spread awareness of the mission's significance. Encourage friends, family, and colleagues to visit the mission and explore its history. Educational outreach and community engagement are key to preserving the mission's legacy, and your advocacy can play a vital role in this effort.

Visiting Mission San Juan Capistrano offers an opportunity to reflect on broader historical and cultural themes. The mission's history encapsulates critical aspects of colonization, cultural exchange, and resilience. By examining these themes, you gain insights into contemporary issues related to cultural preservation, heritage, and identity.

The mission's legacy prompts important questions about how we remember and interpret history, the impact of cultural interactions, and the ways in which historical sites can foster community and identity. Engaging with these reflections enhances your understanding of the mission's enduring relevance and its role in shaping both past and present.

Mission San Juan Capistrano stands as a beacon of historical and cultural significance, inviting you to explore its rich heritage and connect with the stories of those who came before us. Whether through educational programs, cultural celebrations, preservation efforts, or personal reflection, your engagement with the mission enriches your understanding of California's history and its diverse cultural landscape.

By visiting Mission San Juan Capistrano, you become part of its ongoing story, contributing to the preservation and celebration of a site that holds profound historical importance. The mission's enduring legacy serves as a reminder of the resilience and adaptability of the human spirit, encouraging us to honor and learn from the past as we move forward into the future.

Timeline of Events

Timeline of Events

1700s

- **1769**: Spanish exploration of Alta California begins, led by Gaspar de Portolá and Father Junípero Serra. This marks the beginning of the Spanish mission system in California.
- **November 1, 1776**: Mission San Juan Capistrano is founded by Father Junípero Serra. It becomes the seventh of the 21 California missions.
- **1777**: The first adobe church at Mission San Juan Capistrano is completed, providing a place of worship for the mission community.
- **1791**: Construction begins on a larger adobe church to accommodate the growing mission population, reflecting the mission's prosperity.
- **1794**: The mission's population grows significantly, with over 1,000 neophytes (indigenous converts) living and working at the mission.
- **1797**: Construction of the Great Stone Church, an ambitious architectural project, begins. The church is designed to be one of the most impressive structures in the mission system.

1800s

- **1806**: The Great Stone Church is completed and dedicated. It becomes known for its grand design and is a central place of worship for the mission community.
- **December 8, 1812**: A devastating earthquake strikes, severely damaging the Great Stone Church. The bell tower collapses during a Sunday Mass,

resulting in significant loss of life and leaving the church in ruins.

- **1821**: Mexico gains independence from Spain, and California becomes part of the Mexican territory. This political change begins to affect the missions.
- **1833**: The Mexican Congress passes the Secularization Act, aimed at transferring mission properties from the Church to private ownership and integrating indigenous populations into Mexican society.
- **1834**: Mission San Juan Capistrano is secularized. Lands are redistributed, and many mission buildings begin to fall into disrepair due to lack of maintenance and resources.
- **1845**: Governor Pío Pico sells the mission buildings and land to private individuals as part of the secularization process. The mission's religious and community functions are further diminished.
- **1848**: The Treaty of Guadalupe Hidalgo ends the Mexican-American War, and California becomes a U.S. territory. This transition marks another significant change in the region's governance and development.

1900s

- **1910**: Father John O'Sullivan arrives at Mission San Juan Capistrano and is struck by its dilapidated state. He initiates restoration efforts, focusing on preserving the mission's historical and cultural significance.
- **1912**: The first Swallows' Day celebration is held, celebrating the legendary return of the swallows to the mission each spring. This event becomes an annual tradition.

- **1933**: Mission San Juan Capistrano is designated a California Historical Landmark, providing legal protections and recognizing its historical importance.
- **1939**: The Landmarks Club of Southern California, founded by Charles Fletcher Lummis, contributes significantly to the restoration efforts, helping to stabilize and repair mission structures.
- **1946**: The Great Stone Church is partially restored to prevent further deterioration, preserving its ruins as a historic site.
- **1971**: Mission San Juan Capistrano is added to the National Register of Historic Places, highlighting its national significance and aiding in its preservation efforts.
- **1980s**: Major restoration projects are undertaken, including the preservation of the Serra Chapel, one of the oldest buildings in continuous use in California, and other mission structures.

2000s

- **2000**: Restoration efforts continue with significant projects aimed at preserving the mission's historical integrity and enhancing its educational and cultural programs.
- **2010**: The mission celebrates the 100th anniversary of Father John O'Sullivan's arrival and the beginning of its modern restoration era. Commemorative events and exhibits highlight his contributions.
- **2012**: The mission commemorates the 100th Swallows' Day Parade, celebrating this unique tradition that attracts visitors from around the world.

- **2015**: New educational programs and interactive exhibits are launched, offering visitors innovative ways to engage with the mission's history and cultural heritage.
- **2020**: The mission adapts to contemporary challenges by expanding its digital outreach and virtual educational programs, ensuring continued access to its resources despite global disruptions.

Early Influential Figures

Early Influential Figures

Father Junípero Serra

Father Junípero Serra was a Spanish Franciscan friar who played a pivotal role in the establishment of the California mission system. Born on November 24, 1713, in Petra, Mallorca, Spain, Serra entered the Franciscan Order in 1730 and was ordained as a priest in 1737. After teaching philosophy and theology at the University of Palma, he felt a calling to become a missionary. In 1749, he traveled to Mexico, where he spent two decades working in the Sierra Gorda region.

In 1769, Serra joined the expedition led by Gaspar de Portolá to establish Spanish presence in Alta California, an area seen as critical for Spain's colonial ambitions. Serra founded the first mission, San Diego de Alcalá, in 1769. Over the next 15 years, he established a total of nine missions, including Mission San Juan Capistrano on November 1, 1776.

Serra's mission at San Juan Capistrano was initially founded on October 30, 1775, but was temporarily abandoned due to conflicts with the local indigenous people. It was re-established in 1776 after Serra returned with additional support. Serra's work at the missions focused on converting the local Native American population to Christianity, teaching them European agricultural practices, and integrating them into Spanish colonial society. His methods, however, were often harsh and have been criticized for their impact on indigenous cultures and populations.

Father Serra's legacy is complex, marked by his dedication to his mission and the significant cultural and

148

demographic changes he brought to California. He was beatified by Pope John Paul II in 1988 and canonized by Pope Francis in 2015, a recognition that sparked controversy due to the impact of the missions on Native American communities.

Father Fermín Francisco de Lasuén

Father Fermín Francisco de Lasuén was another key figure in the California mission system. Born on July 7, 1736, in Vitoria, Spain, Lasuén joined the Franciscan Order and, like Serra, felt called to missionary work in the Americas. He arrived in Mexico in 1759 and eventually joined the missionary efforts in Alta California.

Lasuén became the second president of the California missions after Father Serra's death in 1784. His leadership was instrumental in the continued expansion and consolidation of the mission system. During his tenure, he founded nine additional missions, bringing the total number of missions to 18. Under his guidance, Mission San Juan Capistrano continued to develop and grow, benefiting from his administrative skills and dedication.

Lasuén focused on improving the living conditions and agricultural productivity of the missions. He implemented irrigation systems, introduced new crops, and improved livestock breeding, which helped the missions become more self-sufficient and prosperous. Lasuén's efforts also extended to the education and conversion of the indigenous populations, continuing Serra's work but often with a more pragmatic and less stringent approach.

Father Lasuén's tenure was marked by a more diplomatic approach to dealing with the Spanish colonial authorities and the local indigenous populations. His leadership ensured the survival and growth of the missions during a critical period of their development. He died on June 26, 1803, leaving behind a legacy of significant contributions to the mission system in California.

Father Vicente Fustér

Father Vicente Fustér was one of the original missionaries at Mission San Juan Capistrano and played a vital role in its early development and operations. His exact birth date and early life details are less documented, but his contributions to the mission are well-recognized.

Fustér arrived in Alta California with the missionary cohort and quickly became involved in the establishment and management of the missions. At San Juan Capistrano, he worked alongside Father Serra and later Father Lasuén, helping to build the mission's infrastructure and community. His work included constructing buildings, organizing agricultural activities, and facilitating the integration of the local indigenous population into the mission system.

Father Fustér was known for his hands-on approach and dedication to the mission's daily operations. He played a significant role in teaching agricultural techniques and European craftsmanship to the Native Americans, contributing to the mission's self-sufficiency and economic stability. His efforts in developing the mission's orchards, vineyards, and livestock herds were particularly noteworthy.

Fustér's tenure at San Juan Capistrano was marked by a commitment to the mission's spiritual and material growth. He worked tirelessly to ensure the mission's success, often dealing with the challenges of limited resources and occasional resistance from the indigenous population. His contributions were integral to the early establishment and functioning of Mission San Juan Capistrano.

Father Vicente Fustér continued his missionary work in California until his death in 1819, leaving a lasting impact on the missions he served and the communities he helped build.

José Antonio Yorba

José Antonio Yorba was a Spanish soldier and landowner who played a significant role in the development of the region surrounding Mission San Juan Capistrano. Born in Catalonia, Spain, in 1746, Yorba joined the Spanish military and eventually participated in the Portolá expedition of 1769, which explored and mapped parts of California, laying the groundwork for future missions.

After his military service, Yorba received a substantial land grant from the Spanish government. This grant, known as Rancho Santiago de Santa Ana, became one of the first and largest ranchos in California, supporting cattle ranching and agriculture. The prosperity of Yorba's rancho contributed to the economic stability of the region, supporting Mission San Juan Capistrano by providing food, livestock, and other resources. His descendants continued to influence Southern California, with the rancho's contributions being pivotal to the mission's success.

Juan Crespí

Juan Crespí was a Spanish Franciscan missionary and one of the earliest chroniclers of California. Born in Mallorca in 1721, Crespí joined the Franciscan Order and was later selected to accompany the Portolá expedition of 1769. His detailed diaries and observations provide invaluable insights into the early exploration and settlement of California.

Crespí meticulously documented the journey of the Portolá expedition, including landscapes, indigenous peoples, and potential sites for future missions. His records were instrumental in the planning and establishment of several missions, including San Juan Capistrano. Although Crespí did not directly establish Mission San Juan Capistrano, his earlier work and detailed documentation provided essential information that facilitated its founding.

Father José Francisco de Paula Señan

Father José Francisco de Paula Señan was a Spanish Franciscan missionary who significantly influenced the development of several California missions, including Mission San Juan Capistrano. Born in Spain in 1760, Señan joined the Franciscan Order and was later sent to the California mission field.

Arriving at Mission San Juan Capistrano in the early 1800s, Father Señan worked diligently to enhance its infrastructure, agricultural production, and educational programs for the indigenous population. Known for his administrative skills, he oversaw the construction of new buildings, expansion of farmlands, and implementation of irrigation systems that boosted agricultural productivity. His efforts helped ensure the mission's self-sufficiency and sustainability, leaving a lasting legacy on the missions he served.

Father St. John O'Sullivan

Father St. John O'Sullivan was born on May 28, 1874, in Louisville, Kentucky. He was ordained as a priest in 1904 after studying theology in Belgium. In the early 20th century, he moved to Southern California, where he initially served in parishes in Los Angeles.

In 1910, Father O'Sullivan was diagnosed with tuberculosis, a condition that led him to seek a more healthful climate. He moved to Mission San Juan Capistrano, hoping the mild weather would improve his health. At that time, the mission was in a state of significant disrepair, with many of its structures crumbling and overgrown.

Father O'Sullivan dedicated himself to the restoration of the mission. With a deep appreciation for history and architecture, he set about repairing the buildings, reviving the gardens, and restoring the overall aesthetic of the mission to reflect its historical significance. His efforts were instrumental in preserving the mission for future generations.

Father O'Sullivan's work at Mission San Juan Capistrano transformed it from a decaying relic into a vibrant historical site. He also initiated the tradition of the "Return of the Swallows," celebrating the annual migration of cliff swallows to the mission. His dedication to preservation and historical education ensured that the mission remained a central part of California's cultural heritage. Father O'Sullivan passed away in 1933, but his legacy lives on in the beautifully restored mission that continues to attract visitors from around the world.

Richard Henry Dana Jr.

Richard Henry Dana Jr. was born on August 1, 1815, in Cambridge, Massachusetts. He was a Harvard student who took a two-year hiatus from his studies due to health issues. During this time, he signed up as a sailor on a merchant ship bound for California.

In 1840, Dana published "Two Years Before the Mast," a memoir that chronicled his voyage from Boston to California and back, between 1834 and 1836. The book provides one of the earliest and most vivid accounts of life in California during the Mexican era. His detailed observations include descriptions of the Californian missions, the landscape, and the daily lives of the inhabitants.

Dana's visit to Mission San Juan Capistrano is particularly noteworthy. He described the mission as a significant landmark and provided valuable insights into its operations and the lives of the people who lived and worked there. His accounts highlight the architectural beauty of the mission and the challenges it faced during that period.

Dana's work remains an important historical document that offers a rare glimpse into California's past. "Two Years

Before the Mast" is still widely read today and serves as a key resource for historians studying the early history of California and its missions. Dana's contribution to the historical context of Mission San Juan Capistrano is invaluable, providing a firsthand account of the mission during a pivotal time in its history.

Helen Hunt Jackson

Helen Hunt Jackson was born Helen Maria Fiske on October 15, 1830, in Amherst, Massachusetts. She became a prominent author and advocate for Native American rights. After the death of her first husband and her two sons, she married William Jackson and took his surname.

In 1884, Jackson published "Ramona," a novel set in Southern California during the mid-19th century. The story revolves around a half-Native American, half-Scottish orphan girl named Ramona, who experiences the struggles and injustices faced by Native Americans in California. While a work of fiction, "Ramona" brought significant attention to the plight of Native Americans and the missions.

"Ramona" played a crucial role in raising public awareness about the California missions, including Mission San Juan Capistrano. The novel's romanticized portrayal of mission life and its historical backdrop sparked renewed interest in these sites. Many readers were inspired to visit the missions, which in turn helped drive efforts to preserve and restore them.

Helen Hunt Jackson's "Ramona" remains a beloved classic and a pivotal work in American literature. Its impact on the preservation and appreciation of the California missions cannot be overstated. Jackson's novel helped to cement Mission San Juan Capistrano's place in the cultural and historical landscape of California, ensuring that the mission would be recognized and preserved as an essential part of the state's heritage.

These three individuals—Father St. John O'Sullivan, Richard Henry Dana Jr., and Helen Hunt Jackson—each played a significant role in the history and preservation of Mission San Juan Capistrano through their unique contributions and enduring legacies.

Governor Felipe de Neve

Governor Felipe de Neve served as the Spanish governor of Alta California from 1775 to 1782. His tenure was marked by a strong commitment to expanding and stabilizing Spanish influence in the region, with the mission system playing a central role in this strategy. De Neve recognized the critical importance of the missions not only as religious centers but also as hubs for economic activity and cultural assimilation of the indigenous populations.

One of his significant contributions was providing essential military and logistical support to the missions, ensuring their protection and sustainability. He understood that the security of the missions was paramount to their success, and thus, he strategically positioned military presidios (forts) to defend these outposts from potential threats, including indigenous resistance and foreign incursions.

Governor de Neve also introduced the Reglamento de Gobierno, a set of regulations aimed at improving the governance and economic management of the missions and presidios. These regulations were designed to make the missions more self-sufficient, reducing their dependency on the military for supplies and support. By enforcing these rules, de Neve sought to create a more stable and prosperous mission system.

His policies and support were instrumental in the foundation and growth of Mission San Juan Capistrano. The security provided by the military presence under his governance allowed the mission to develop without the constant threat of attacks. Governor de Neve's legacy is evident in the success and endurance of the mission system, which continued to function as centers of agriculture, education, and religious instruction long after his tenure.

Eulalia Pérez de Guillén Mariné

Eulalia Pérez de Guillén Mariné played a unique and significant role at Mission San Juan Capistrano as the housekeeper and mayordoma (head housekeeper). Born in 1766 in Loreto, Baja California, she moved to Alta California, where she became deeply involved in the daily operations of the missions, especially San Juan Capistrano and later Mission San Gabriel.

Eulalia provided some of the most detailed and personal accounts of daily life at the California missions during the early 19th century. Her recollections, often shared in her later years, offer invaluable insights into the social, cultural, and economic aspects of mission life. She described everything from the routines of food preparation and household management to the intricacies of religious practices and the dynamics between the missionaries, settlers, and the indigenous population.

Her oral histories, recorded by historians and anthropologists, have become a rich primary source for understanding the inner workings of the missions. Eulalia's detailed memories help paint a vivid picture of life at the missions, highlighting the roles of women, the labor of the indigenous people, and the overall environment of the mission community. Her contributions are invaluable for providing a human perspective on the mission era, bringing to life the experiences of those who lived and worked there.

José Francisco Ortega

José Francisco Ortega was a prominent Spanish soldier and early settler who played a crucial role in the history of Mission San Juan Capistrano. Born in 1734 in Celaya, Guanajuato, New Spain, he joined the Spanish military and became a key figure in the exploration and colonization of Alta California.

Ortega was a member of the Portolá expedition in 1769, the first European land expedition to explore the area that would become California. His skills as an explorer and soldier were instrumental in the early stages of Spanish colonization. He later served as the comandante (commander) of various presidios, including those at San Diego and Santa Barbara, providing military support to the missions.

His leadership and experience were vital in ensuring the safety and security of the missions during their early years. Ortega's presence helped to establish a stable environment in which the missions, including San Juan Capistrano, could flourish. He also played a role in fostering relations with the indigenous peoples, navigating the complex dynamics between the Spanish settlers and the native communities.

Ortega's contributions to the mission system and his role in the exploration and settlement of California left a lasting impact on the region. His efforts helped lay the groundwork for the successful establishment and growth of the missions, securing their place in California's history.

Charles Lummis

Charles Lummis, a notable journalist and historian, played a crucial role in the preservation of California's missions, including Mission San Juan Capistrano. Born in 1859, Lummis was a man of many talents, including writer, editor, and advocate for Native American rights. His passion for the history and culture of the American Southwest led him to become a fervent supporter of the mission preservation movement. Lummis' work was instrumental in raising public awareness about the historical significance of the missions. Through his writings and public speaking, he highlighted the cultural and architectural importance of these sites, garnering support for their preservation at a time when many were falling into disrepair. His efforts helped to ensure that the missions, including San Juan Capistrano, were recognized as vital pieces of California's heritage, leading to increased efforts to restore and maintain them for future generations.

Frances W. Lathrop

Frances W. Lathrop, an early 20th-century historian, emerged as a dedicated advocate for the preservation of Mission San Juan Capistrano. Lathrop's work was pivotal during a period when the mission was at risk of being lost to neglect and decay. Her scholarly approach to the history of the mission, combined with her passionate advocacy, brought attention to the need for preservation. Lathrop's detailed research and publications on the mission's history provided a foundation for future restoration efforts. She worked tirelessly to gather support from both the public and private sectors, emphasizing the mission's historical and cultural importance. Her efforts not only helped secure funding for restoration projects but also inspired a new generation of historians and preservationists to continue the work she had started.

Adelaide Hahn

Adelaide Hahn was another key figure in the preservation and restoration of Mission San Juan Capistrano during the 20th century. Known for her meticulous attention to detail and deep appreciation for historical architecture, Hahn played a significant role in the ongoing efforts to restore the mission to its former glory. Her contributions were not limited to physical restoration; she also worked to educate the public about the mission's historical significance. Hahn's efforts included organizing community events, fundraising campaigns, and educational programs that aimed to foster a greater appreciation for the mission among local residents and visitors alike. Her dedication to the mission's preservation ensured that its historical structures were not only restored but also maintained, preserving the integrity and authenticity of this historical landmark for future generations to enjoy.

These modern contributors, through their dedication and hard work, played indispensable roles in the preservation and restoration of Mission San Juan Capistrano. Their combined efforts have helped to ensure that this iconic piece of California's history remains a vibrant and cherished landmark, accessible to all who wish to explore its rich past.

Harry Downie

Harry Downie was a pivotal figure in the 20th-century restoration efforts of Mission San Juan Capistrano. Born in San Francisco in 1903, Downie developed an early interest in California history and architecture. He is best known for his meticulous restoration work across the California mission system, with San Juan Capistrano being one of his most significant projects.

Downie began his career with the California mission restorations in the 1930s. His work was characterized by a deep respect for historical accuracy and authenticity. At Mission San Juan Capistrano, he undertook extensive research to ensure that the restoration would faithfully reflect the original construction and aesthetics of the mission as it was in the late 18th and early 19th centuries. Downie's efforts included the reconstruction of original adobe buildings, preservation of historic artifacts, and the careful restoration of the mission's iconic bell wall and gardens.

Downie's dedication to preserving the missions was not only about physical restoration but also about educating the public. He worked closely with historians, archaeologists, and local communities to promote the mission's cultural and historical significance. His work has left a lasting legacy, making the missions, including San Juan Capistrano, some of the best-preserved examples of Spanish colonial architecture in the United States.

C.C. Chapman

Charles C. Chapman, commonly known as C.C. Chapman, was an influential historian whose work significantly contributed to the documentation of California's Spanish period, including detailed histories of its missions. Born in 1853, Chapman was a scholar with a deep interest in California's early history. His most notable work, "A History of California: The Spanish Period," published in 1921, remains a seminal text for understanding the era.

Chapman's book provides a comprehensive overview of California during the Spanish colonial period, meticulously detailing the establishment and development of the missions. His work is particularly valuable for its thorough research and use of primary sources, including diaries, letters, and official records. In his detailed accounts of Mission San Juan Capistrano, Chapman describes the mission's founding, its architectural evolution, and its role in the local economy and society.

Chapman's historical writings helped to elevate the importance of California's mission history in the broader context of American history. His scholarship has been crucial for historians, educators, and preservationists working to maintain the legacy of the missions.

Bancroft Family

The Bancroft family, particularly Hubert Howe Bancroft, played a crucial role in documenting the history of California and its missions. Hubert Howe Bancroft (1832-1918) was an American historian and ethnologist who amassed one of the largest collections of historical materials on the American West, including an extensive collection on California's missions.

Bancroft's collection included books, manuscripts, maps, and personal accounts that provided an unparalleled resource for historians. His work, "The Works of Hubert Howe Bancroft," a 39-volume series, includes comprehensive histories of the Spanish period in California. The volumes cover a wide range of topics, from the establishment of missions to the daily lives of missionaries and Native Americans.

Bancroft's meticulous documentation and archival efforts preserved invaluable historical information that might have otherwise been lost. His dedication to preserving and studying California's mission history laid the groundwork for future historians and ensured that the stories of places like Mission San Juan Capistrano would be remembered and studied for generations.

The Bancroft family's contribution extended beyond Hubert, as his collection eventually became the foundation of the Bancroft Library at the University of California, Berkeley. This institution continues to be a vital resource for researchers studying the history of California and the American West.

Together, Harry Downie, C.C. Chapman, and the Bancroft family have each played significant roles in preserving, documenting, and promoting the rich history of Mission San Juan Capistrano, ensuring its legacy endures.

Glossary

Glossary

Acjachemen (Juaneño)

The indigenous people who inhabited the area around Mission San Juan Capistrano long before the arrival of the Spanish. Known as the Juaneño by the Spanish, the Acjachemen had a rich culture and society that was significantly impacted by the establishment of the mission.

Adobe

A building material made from earth and organic materials such as straw. Adobe bricks were commonly used in the construction of mission buildings, including those at Mission San Juan Capistrano.

Alta California

The name given by the Spanish to the region that now comprises the state of California. It was part of the Viceroyalty of New Spain until Mexican independence in 1821.

Baptism

A Christian sacrament of initiation and purification. The Spanish missionaries performed baptisms on the indigenous people, marking their conversion to Christianity and their formal entry into the mission community.

Bell Tower

A structure housing bells, often used to call people to worship or signal important events. The bell tower of the Great Stone Church at Mission San Juan Capistrano collapsed during an earthquake in 1812, leading to significant loss of life.

California Historical Landmark

A designation given to buildings, structures, sites, or places that have historical significance. Mission San Juan Capistrano received this designation in 1933.

Catechism

Religious instruction based on a set of questions and answers. The Spanish missionaries taught catechism to the indigenous people as part of their efforts to convert them to Christianity.

Convento

The residential quarters for the missionaries at a mission. At Mission San Juan Capistrano, the Convento wing includes the long arcaded corridor that is one of the mission's most photographed features.

Dovecote

A structure intended to house pigeons or doves. Mission San Juan Capistrano has a historic dovecote that was used to raise pigeons for food and other purposes.

El Camino Real

Spanish for "The Royal Road," this was a network of roads that connected the California missions, including Mission San Juan Capistrano, facilitating travel and communication between them.

Father Junípero Serra

A Spanish Franciscan friar who founded the California mission system. Father Serra established Mission San Juan Capistrano in 1776 as part of his efforts to convert the indigenous peoples to Christianity.

Franciscans

Members of the Catholic religious order founded by St. Francis of Assisi. The Franciscan friars were responsible for establishing and running the California missions, including Mission San Juan Capistrano.

Great Stone Church

An impressive stone church constructed at Mission San Juan Capistrano beginning in 1797. It was destroyed by an earthquake in 1812, and its ruins are a significant historical and architectural feature of the mission.

Juaneño

The name given by the Spanish to the Acjachemen people who lived in the area around Mission San Juan Capistrano.

This term is derived from the mission's patron saint, St. John (San Juan).

Mission System

A chain of 21 religious and military outposts established by Spanish Catholics of the Franciscan Order between 1769 and 1833 in what is now California. The mission system aimed to spread Christianity among the indigenous peoples and consolidate Spanish territorial claims.

Neophyte

A new convert to Christianity, specifically referring to the indigenous people who were converted by the Spanish missionaries at the California missions.

Plaza

A central open space or public square. The plaza at Mission San Juan Capistrano served as a communal area for religious, social, and economic activities.

Secularization

The process of transferring property and responsibilities from the Church to the civil authorities. In California, the missions were secularized by the Mexican government beginning in 1833, leading to the redistribution of mission lands and resources.

St. Joseph's Day

March 19, the feast day of St. Joseph, which is traditionally associated with the return of the swallows to Mission San Juan Capistrano. This day is celebrated with various events and festivities at the mission.

Swallows

Migratory birds famous for their annual return to Mission San Juan Capistrano around St. Joseph's Day. This natural phenomenon has become a celebrated event and symbol of the mission.

Vaquero

A Spanish term for a cowboy or cattle herder. Vaqueros played a significant role in the livestock operations at the California missions, including Mission San Juan Capistrano.

Viceroyalty of New Spain

A Spanish colonial territory that included present-day Mexico, Central America, and parts of the southwestern United States, including California. Mission San Juan Capistrano was established during the period when Alta California was part of the Viceroyalty of New Spain.

Sources and References

Sources and References

Books

- Beebe, Rose Marie, and Robert M. Senkewicz. *Junípero Serra: California, Indians, and the Transformation of a Missionary*. University of Oklahoma Press, 2015.
- Bolton, Herbert Eugene. *Fray Juan Crespi: Missionary Explorer on the Pacific Coast, 1769-1774*. University of California Press, 1927.
- Engelhardt, Zephyrin. *San Juan Capistrano Mission*. Standard Printing Co., 1922.
- Kelsey, Harry. *Mission San Juan Capistrano: A Pocket History*. Historical Commission, 1995.
- Leffingwell, Randy. *California Missions and Presidios: The History and Beauty of the Spanish Missions*. Voyageur Press, 2005.
- Milliken, Randall. *A Time of Little Choice: The Disintegration of Tribal Culture in the San Francisco Bay Area 1769-1810*. Ballena Press, 1995.
- Phillips, George Harwood. *Indians and Intruders in Central California, 1769-1849*. University of Oklahoma Press, 1993.

Articles

- Castillo, Edward D. "Short Overview of California Indian History." *California Native American Heritage Commission*. https://nahc.ca.gov/resources/california-indian-history/.

- Hackel, Steven W. "From Mission to Municipality: The Political and Economic Transition of Mission San Juan Capistrano after Secularization." *Southern California Quarterly*, vol. 89, no. 1, 2007, pp. 1-34.
- Jackson, Robert H., and Edward Castillo. "Indians, Franciscans, and Spanish Colonization: The Impact of the Mission System on California Indians." *The Western Historical Quarterly*, vol. 25, no. 1, 1994, pp. 1-30.

Websites

- California Missions Foundation. "Mission San Juan Capistrano." *California Missions*. https://californiamissionsfoundation.org/the-missions/mission-san-juan-capistrano/.
- Mission San Juan Capistrano. "History of the Mission." *Mission San Juan Capistrano*. https://www.missionsjc.com/history-of-the-mission/.
- National Park Service. "San Juan Capistrano Mission." *National Register of Historic Places*. https://www.nps.gov/places/san-juan-capistrano-mission.htm.
- The California Missions Resource Center. "Mission San Juan Capistrano." *California Missions Resource Center*. https://www.missionscalifornia.com/keyfacts/mission-san-juan-capistrano.

Reports

- California Department of Parks and Recreation. *Mission San Juan Capistrano: Archaeological Investigations and Historical Research*. California Department of Parks and Recreation, 2001.

- San Juan Capistrano Historical Society. *San Juan Capistrano: Historical and Archaeological Reports.* San Juan Capistrano Historical Society, 2010.

Theses and Dissertations

- Smith, Andrew. "Cultural Interactions at Mission San Juan Capistrano: An Archaeological Perspective." PhD diss., University of California, Berkeley, 2012.
- Rodriguez, Marisol. "The Impact of Secularization on the Indigenous Population of San Juan Capistrano." Master's thesis, California State University, Fullerton, 2008.

Multimedia

- Public Broadcasting Service (PBS). *California Missions: San Juan Capistrano.* Directed by Michael Murphy, PBS, 2005.
- The Huntington Library. *Voices of the Mission: Oral Histories from San Juan Capistrano.* Audio recordings, The Huntington Library, 2010.

Author's Note

Author's Note

Dear Reader,

Thank you for embarking on this journey through the history of Mission San Juan Capistrano with me. Your interest in this remarkable place is deeply appreciated, and I hope that you have found this book both informative and inspiring.

As a native of Southern California, I have always felt a profound connection to the special places that define our region. Mission San Juan Capistrano stands out not only as the "Jewel of the Missions" but also as a true treasure for all of California. Its story is one of beauty and resilience, marked by periods of growth, decline, and renewal. The mission has played a tumultuous role in the history of our state, reflecting the broader changes and challenges that have shaped California.

It is important to remember that the history of Mission San Juan Capistrano, and indeed all of California, began with the indigenous peoples who first inhabited this land. The Acjachemen people, known as the Juaneño, were the original stewards of this region. Their culture, traditions, and contributions are an integral part of the mission's story. This was their land long before the arrival of the Spanish, and it will always be their land.

I am profoundly grateful to the Acjachemen people for allowing me to tell their stories and share their history. Their resilience and adaptability in the face of profound change are testaments to their enduring spirit. It is my hope that this book honors their legacy and helps to preserve their rich cultural heritage for future generations.

Thank you once again for your time and interest. By learning about and appreciating the history of Mission San Juan Capistrano, you are helping to ensure that this precious jewel continues to shine brightly for many years to come.

Much love,

Logan Stover

Logan Stover is an Author, Historian, & Special Education Teacher from Southern California

www.LoganStover.com
Explore Logan's Other Books
Amazon – eBay - Etsy

Made in the USA
Las Vegas, NV
01 March 2025